"ABUSE TI

"IGNORE WOMEN RIGHTS
(Timothy 2:12)

"AND GET RID OF GAYS, AND THE POOR AND WOMEN WHO DO NOT FOLLOW OUR BIBLE"
(Leviticus 20:13, Deuteronomy 17:12 and 22:21, 2Chronicles 15:13
Source: www.biblehub.com)

"I am the U.S. President, and I approve of this message"

"We are the Supreme Court Justices, and we also

approve of this message"

"We are Senators, and we approve these messages too"

"We all are sworn onto the Bible, committed to commit

it... not to quit it"

PRAISING CRIMES

.....*"You may Kidnap male and female from nations that are around you". "The Kidnapped ought to be beaten with blows if not obeying their masters". "Everything that is written in Bible must be fulfilled. Not an iota or a dot is to be missed from the commands". "And if you do not obey and do not carry out the commands, God will destroy you, make you blind, make you eat the flesh of your sons and daughters, enslave you, etc".*

(Leviticus 25:44, Luke 12: 47, Matthew, 5:18, Leviticus 26:16 and 26:29).

In the United States Kidnapping, torturing, killing and genocide are respected by high rank officials! The officials are sworn into office by a book that commands to its followers to commit violent crimes! Not only they value the Unconstitutional context of the book above all that of the Constitution, but also they make commitment to fulfill the threatening commands! Their gesture, advertises one particular religion that promotes violence, racism, hallucination and psychopathy, and induces and persuades others to engage in hate crimes:

Racism and Violence:
Bible: Luke: 12:47 "Beat the Black in the Back" (If slaves do not follow their masters' command, they must be beaten severely).
Bible: Colossians 3:22 *"Slaves, in all things obey those who are your masters on earth... with sincerity of heart, fearing the Lord"*.
Deuteronomy, 22:21 *"Kill your women if she is liberal"* *(Stone her to death if found not to be virgin)*.
2Chronicles 15:13 *"You shall stone them to death, the man or woman who has done the evil serving other gods"*.

Corinthians 6:9 *"Homosexuals do not inherit the kingdom of God"*.

Leviticus 20:13 *"If a man lies with a male as with a woman, both of them shall be put to death"*.

Exodus 22:18 *"You shall not allow a sorceress to live"*.

Revelation 2:23 *"And I will kill her children with poison"*.

Revelation 2:27 *"And he shall rule them with a Rod of Iron"*.

Hallucination and Psychopathy:

Revelation 6:13 *"And the Stars of the sky fell to the Earth, as a fig tree casts its unripe figs shaken by a great* wind."

Revelation 10:10 *"And I ate the book"*.

For thousands of years, the rulers of religious run states applied the fundamental ideology of the Bible as the constituted law to maintain their ruling status. Based on the schizophrenic preaching of the book, they tortured and executed other races, genders and believers. Even scientists and writers were not safe from prosecution for representing their scientific research. Thousands of teenage girls burnt alive in the fire for praying to other Gods and thousands of intellectuals prosecuted for their

4

true findings by the hands of those who had their hands on the Bible. Whoever said the Earth was round was bound for Guillotine. Homosexuals, Women, Sorcerers, magicians, entertainers and dancers, who were mostly women, prosecuted and executed because the Christian States referred to the verses of their Bible as their constituted law to administer justice and rule over people. The very same book, which was the measure of law for the ruthless religious monarchs who committed mass murder, is given recognition today by the State that is meant to be secular! The influence of the superstitious teaching of the book for hundreds of years could not have vanished from the minds of the U.S. revolutionaries in such a short time (From 1773 to 1776). And because of the preaching of the book that confirmed Slavery:

Leviticus 25:44 *"You may acquire male and female slaves from pagan nations that are around you."*
The Kidnapping of people continued for another 89 years (1776-1865). Leaders such as General Lee, George Washington, or chief justice Roger Taney, who solemnly swore to the Bible to administer justice "without respect"

to persons, respected their prophets' words that disrespected the Kidnapped people:

Titus 2:9 *"Urge the bond slaves to be subject to their masters in everything, to be well-pleasing, not argumentative, nor pilfering/stealing..."*
Luke 12:47 *"The servant who knows the master's will and does not do what the master wants will be beaten with many blows."*

Chief justice Roger Taney: *"Slaves are to serve their masters. They can't be citizens"*.
General Lee: *"Lay it well"* (Referring to the lashes)
George Washington: *"They are wretched creatures"*.

Matthew 26:30 *"Throw out the worthless slave into the outer darkness"*.

The leaders of the county, at such high ranks, did ordered the cruel punishments of flogging of people from "pagan nations" and they did Kidnapped "the worthless slave into the outer darkness" because they respected few persons' ideology rather than respecting the beliefs of millions that constituted into law.

Officials, who have been performing the rituals of their Sect by resting their left hand on the Bible, and raising their right hand (Like Hitler salute), have been respecting the idea of the few of their religious leaders over the ideas of millions of people in administering justice. They have been legislating laws in favor of their prophets and executing and administering justice "with respects" to such persons. They have been respecting verses that violate the Constitution for the last 244 years. Many judges choose to favor their judgment toward their religious political groups to secure their political and financial status. By their approval of such persons of Paul and John, the officials respect other persons in their Oath and by doing so, they automatically nullify their Oath because they are sworn in to administer justice *without* respect to *persons* but they respect the religious figures right at their Oath!

Title 28, 453. *OATHS OF JUSTICES AND JUDGES: Each justice or Judge of the United States shall take the* *following oath or affirmation before performing the duties of his office: "I, ___ ___, do solemnly swear (or affirm) that I will administer justice **without** respect to persons, and do equal right to the poor and to the rich, and that I will faithfully and impartially discharge and perform all the duties incumbent upon me as ___ under the Constitution and laws of the United States. So help me God."*

The muscular leaders respected the muscular sex of prophets, priests, pastors and reverends who preached the disrespectful preaching toward many others, especially women:

Deuteronomy, 22:21 *"Kill your women if she is not tight"* (Stone her to death if found not to be virgin).

Timothy 2:11 *"A woman must quietly receive instruction with entire submissiveness"*.

Timothy 2:14 *"And it was not Adam who was deceived, but the women being deceived, fell into transgression"*. (Referring to Eve).

Colossians 3 *"Wives, be subject to your husbands, as is fitting in the Lord"*.

The fathers of our nation could not have allowed the mothers of our nation to participate in Government because:

Deuteronomy, 25:12 *"You shall cut off her hand"* (The hand of the wife who intervenes in his husband's fight and grabs the genitals of the man who is fighting with his husband).

Galatians 4:22 through 4:*31 "Cast out the bondwoman (Slave woman) and her son, for the son of the bondwoman shall not be an heir with the son of the free woman. We are not children of bondwoman, but of the free woman."* (Referring to Ibrahim, who is said to have children from her captive wife as well as none captive wife. Israelites are to be free because they are the descendants of the free woman, and nations around Israel are from pagan nations who are the descendant of the Captive woman and they cannot be free).

So it took another 144 years for woman rights to be recognized (1776 until 1920). In fact, the Bible delayed the recognition of the rights of women, the Kidnapped

Immigrants and homosexuals for about 2000 years. (The Old Testament delayed it for 4000 years).

Half of the nation were to be shut up for another 144 years simply because the Bible said so:

Timothy 2:12 *"But I do not allow a woman to teach or exercise authority over man, but to remain quiet."*

And just recently and after 239 years, the rights of LGBTs are recognized (Almost) because:

Corinthians 6:9 *"Homosexuals do not inherit the kingdom of God"*.
Leviticus 20:13 *"If a man lies with a male as with a woman, both of them shall be put to death"*.

For the last 243 years, (1776-2019) little by little, the influence of the book's preaching has been fading away and more logic, reasoning, freedom and justice has been taking place. (Equal right to vote, equal usage of buses, water fountains, restaurants and cinemas, equal pay, equal right to serve in army and equal gender marriage and so on). The venomous verses that poisoned the minds for thousands of years could not have been surgically taken out by the sword of the revolutionaries nor could it be cured quickly with anti-venom. The poison that the religion injected into mind, poisoned the body of the society. Organs attacked by the venoms, attacked other Organs. Organizations poisoned by the venom, attacked other organizations within the same body of the society. Groups attacked other groups. They waged wars killing each other over the religion. Organizations literally used poison to poison others' organs of other Organizations! The poisonous minds used poisonous gas of Chlorine in WWI to attack organs of other Organizations because their book said is Ok to poison them and even poison their children:

Bible, Revelation 2:23 *"Kill her children with poison"*.

In World War I, Poisonous gases of Phosgene, Chlorine and Mustard used to kill thousands. Christian German nationals used Poison to eliminate None-Christians or atheists because:

Deuteronomy *"You shall stone them to death, the man or woman who has done the evil serving other gods"*.

Nahum 3:15 *"Fire will consume you, the sword will cut you down"*.

The poisonous word...

That poisoned the world...

The people, who were poisoned by the words, literally poisoned the people of the World!

The prophets poisoned the minds of people. The Sect leaders sickened the minds enough to persuade people to kill groups of other people or even to kill their own groups! (Reverend Jimmy Jones poisoned the minds of their Sect who poisoned themselves killing 900 people in 1978. The Sect of Nazi poisoned None-Christians Socialists and Jews in concentration camps killing millions.) Not only they killed their own but they willing to even destroy the World in order to fulfill their prophet's prophecies; the Armageddon. Their prophets, who were sick themselves having schizophrenia and having illusionary visions and hearing voices, preached against others of being schizophrenic and hearing voices calling them witches and then executed them. They invented the illusionary enemy of devil and they accused groups of people (Mostly women) having devil, demon, evil and Satin in them. Then, the Schizophrenic prophets and priests ordered the execution of their enemies and burned them alive in the fire for the sake of their God:

Exodus 22:18 *"You shall not let a sorceress to live."*

In World War II, Christian nationalists of Germany poisoned people who were in need of mental care and they used them as subjects in their experimental laboratories because Bible does not respect such people to enter the house of God:

Deuteronomy 23 *"No one who is emasculated or has his male organ cut off shall enter the assembly of the Lord".*

The people, who needed special care, were poisoned and burnt in the fire, used as biological subjects in laboratories, electrocuted, or just let to be rotten in the corners of the streets. (In the U.S. they are let to wonder in cities to be raped, selling their body for food, or they are jailed in jail like facilities for treatments. Instead of being provided with group activities such as watching nature and animals, etc. In 1950s, U.S. Government electrocuted those in need of mental care to make them right. Today, many special women with mental care are forced to wonder in the streets and to be raped trading their body for food and shelter to make a living because the leaders of the country believe in the verses of the Bible that consider them committing a sin and having demon who are fooled by the devil and not worthy of being taken care of and saved).

Critics of the Bible and Church were thrown into the fire by priest and religious officials who had their hands on the Bible. (In the U.S. at least 20 people are recorded to be burnt alive in the fire). Officials, who had their hands on the Bible, silenced the critics to secure their religious, political, financial and ruling status. To have access to the resources of nations, land, women, treasure, and slaves, they killed, captured and tortured people to achieve their goals. They used physical force Kidnapping African to use their body, or they used gunpowder, poison or printing paper as currency, to invade, capture, or acquire nations' resources. (Private Banks have been printing toilet paper as money in mass and injecting the paper money into the World economy for 150 years and exchanging their paper with the riches of the World or simply using their paper money to corrupt officials or to create Coup De Ta and oust regimes). To have easy access to the resources of nations and sell weapons and guns, the religious leaders of the Sect create sectorial conflicts among nations overseas and they create racial conflicts within the nation by their acts of espionage, poisoning and wars:

History.state.gov: *unclassified Governmental communications: "b. Poison pen, personal denunciations, rumor spreading, etc.: C.I.A. has means of making fairly effective personal attacks against any political figure in Iran, including Mossadegh."* (1953, Officials designed Poison pens to eliminate democratic leaders of nations to have access to their country's Oil and sell them weapons if their plan of coup de ta were to fail).

For having access to the resources of nations and to profit selling weapons to nations, the Conspirators commit offence against the United States by wasting the lives of thousands of young Americans in the wars that only would profit the owners of Towers and Bank executives in the office (Mnuchin and Trump). For personal gains and to sell Guns and Weapons, they created violence and conflicts inside the country causing the shootings in Casinos, Malls, Clubs, Churches, and Schools and they created violence and conflicts overseas forcing many nations to retaliate against the citizens of the United States by terrorist attacks.

For personal gain, they make people live with fear and pain.

For personal gain, the executives of Private Banking in control of the Treasury, have defrauded the United States trillions of dollars by indebting the nation to their own Private Banks. (In 1913, many corrupt officials, backed by bankers, handed the nation wealth to the Private Banks that called themselves Federal Reserve! To easily print paper as money through loaning the money that they do not even have! And by asking interest on the money they loan, they have made themselves fortunes. They have made a rule for themselves to loan 9 times over of the amount of their actual savings!).

The Statesmen's aggression toward people is been reduced, but their seal of abuse is still in use. The Bible is there and the Statesmen still promote the Seal. They still Symbolize the Seal.

Revelation 7:4 *"One hundred and forty –four thousand sealed from every tribe of the sons of Israel"*.

The abusive criminal ideology that one group of people are superior to its neighboring countries and they have the right to harm and abuse them is still in use in the Government. The Bible still is sealed to the State and the ideology is still in use in the Government, which respects and promotes the Bible:

Revelation 7:3 *"We have sealed our bond-servants of our God on their foreheads."*

The Bible is there and the Sect ideology have infiltrated in the Republican Party to collect support and to have control over the Treasury, Real states and Banking. The War in Middle East and protecting Israel against nations around it is because the Bible calls Jewish nationals the chosen people and it commands its followers to attack the neighboring nations or to take them as slaves:

Leviticus 26:44 *"You may acquire male and female slaves from pagan nations that are around you"*.

Joel 3:8 *"I will sell your sons and daughters to the people of Judah, and they will sell them to the people of Sabeans"*.

Ezekiel 9:6 *"Slaughter the old men, the young men and women, the mothers and children, but do not touch anyone who has the sealed mark"*.

Ezekiel 9:5 *"Kill everyone in the city whose forehead is not marked. Show no mercy; have no pity"*.

Amos 1:7 *"So I will send fire upon the wall of Gaza and it will consume her citadels."*

Zephaniah 2:12 *"You also, O Ethiopians, will be slain by my sword ""The God of Israel declares"* (2:9).

(The Bible gave free hands to Mussolini to occupy Ethiopia. The war that killed 700,000 Ethiopian of whom half a million were civilians!)

Nahum 3:5 *"Behold, I am against you, declares the Lord; And I will lift up your skirts over your face, and show to the nations your nakedness..."* 3:15 *"Fire will consume you, the* sword will cut you down" (Threatening Syria and Iraq and the mistress of sorceries and harlotries).

Micah 1:6 *"I will make Samaria (West Bank) a heap of ruins in the open country".*

Hosea 13:16 *"Samaria will be held guilty, for she has rebelled against her God. They will fall by the sword, their little one will be dashed in pieces, and their pregnant women will be ripped open.* (O, Jesus! Presidents, Congressmen and Justices respecting such verses! Unbelievable!)

And of course our dear Country, the United States of America, through officials who have their hands on the Bible, support one particular nation and one particular religion against many surrounding nations. And with doing so, the Sect leaders, who have infiltrated into the U.S. political party of Republican, set policies that benefits their Sect and in doing so they persuade Americans and certain nations to attack many other nations and they promote racism inside the country to provoke violence toward the immigrants, whose nationality or race and gender is spoken against by their Bible. For their own profits of selling Guns inside the Country or selling Weapons to other countries, and to profit from their Prophets (Collecting money and votes in Churches) and to increase their assets, they set pro violence policies that endanger the lives of the Citizens of America by creating conflicts among people inside the country and by creating conflicts, wars outside of the country. At times, the Sect sides with one group or one nation to attack other group of people creating sectorial warfare among nations. They provide their favorite Sect with weapons, which could be used to attack other nations including the United States! (Supporting of BAATH of Saddam, Al Qaeda of Ben Laden, and many other groups by the members of the Sect is widely known. Some Republican gave millions of dollars to both Sects to compete with Russia in having access to the region Oil and selling the countries in the region weapons, products and services). The Sect supports their "wholly land" and because they believe in using aggression and violence toward many nations, they make such nations to become the enemy of the United States. They have turned many of other nationals against the United States endangering the lives of millions who do not support the Bible's violent ideology. Innocent people of America are made to fight a war for the members of the Bible-ists. The war that only profits the followers of the Sect who own Towers, Banks, Real States and hold share Stocks in weapon manufacturing.

This is Conspiracy against all American who do not believe in the violent ideology of the Sect while their young children are sent to be killed in the wars that only benefit owners of Towers or the Private Bank executives in control of the Treasury.

The Sect that infiltrated in Republican Party endangers thousands of American lives by turning the whole world against us. They create illusionary enemies of demons, devil, evil and satin in the mind of people so people get use to believe in illusionary enemies and willing to fight the wars with illusionary enemies that they would create for their own profit.

They use their prophets for their profits...

The support of the abusive violent ideology to protect one place as wholly and attacking other nationals and other believers, make such nationals the enemy of the States and cause them to attack Americans in their act of Terrorism.

Both sides, both Secs, who either believe in the Bible or Quran, not only act against each other, but also they act against their own countries to stay in ruling class and to have access to power and the resources of nations in the cost of the loss of thousands of lives. (Russians supporting Iran selling them their weapons and the U.S. supporting Saudi Arabia selling them weapons and sending them to war to use up the weapons and ammunition to supply them again regardless of how many American lives will be lost! In Christian wars among themselves, millions of Christian lives wasted from both sides in Crimean Wars between Catholic Church and Orthodox Church that fought to control the Wholly land! The wars between Shiites and Sonnies wasted millions of lives in their 1400 years of conflicts!)

Quran: *"None believers and infidels are to die."*
Bible, Deuteronomy: *"You shall stone them to death, the man or woman who has done the evil serving other gods"*.

"Everyone who would not seek the lord of Israel is to be put to death". (Chronicles 15:12-13 NAB).

It seems that the crusades will never be over.

The violent preaching...

The violent teaching...

The pray to prey...

The violent verses of the violent teaching continue to cast fear everywhere:

Micah 4:13 *"Arise Zion that you may pulverize many people that you may devote to the Lord..."*

Ezekiel 16:*39 "I will give you into the hands of your lovers and they strip you of your clothing, take away your jewels, and will leave you naked and bare." "They will burn your houses, cut you to pieces with their swords." "So, I will claim my fury against you and my jealousy will depart from you, and I will be pacified and angry no more."*

Quran: "Taking the blood of those who do not believe in your God is sacred".

And both Sects share the common violent and racist persuasion toward women and homosexuals:

Bible, Deuteronomy 22:21 "If your wife is not tight, kill her", "If your wife found not to be virgin, shall be stoned to death."

Quran: *"Beat your wife in bed if she doesn't let you to rape her."*

(Stoning was first invented by Moses; the prophet of Judaism and both Quran and Bible are against homosexuals.)

The symptoms of psychopathic acts of terrorism or shootings in malls, schools or casinos, bombing the Federal building and crashing into the twin towers are caused by the promotion and persuasion of violence, racism and superstitious ideology of the many Sects around the World that poisons the mind causing people to blow themselves up killing others. People would be abused by religions' harsh practices and their life style would be affected by the politicians' violent policies, which cause hardship on people's life by making policies that are based on the harsh and violent preaching of their ideology. The corruption in religion and politics, corrupts the minds of people as well. People are repelled from religion and authorities or rules. Hopeless and goalless in life, the distressed mind, who mostly suffer economically and from family values hates such life and picks up Gun shooting people at public place to end the lives it hates. Like many other violent teaching of many other violent Religious and Nationalist Sects such as: Nazis, BAATH, AL Qaeda, Hezbollah, ISIST, Ikhud, or BoKo Haram, the Religious Nationalist Sect that have infiltrated in Republican Party, uses their book's ideology to attract support and to reach to office and control the Treasury to benefit their Banks and Real Estates. (Like Steven Mnuchin a Banker and Trump a Real Stator) They become violent toward others especially other nationals. Their respect for the violent, racist and schizophrenic teaching of the book prompts the leader of such Sects to become schizophrenic, racist, and to hate, which causes him to seek violence and harm others to get satisfaction. He becomes violent toward others especially other nationals with other beliefs. And then, the sick leader of the Sect seeks war by terrorist attacks. Such as Hitler, Mussolini, Saddam Hossain, Osama ben Laden, Arial Sharon, George Bush, etc. The action of any one of these leaders might look legitimate from the viewpoint of the reader. A person with different nationality, religion or ethnicity who is reading her or his Ex-leader name mentioned as a terrorist may get offended for he or she is influenced by the propaganda to be patriotic to religious- nationalism especially if she or he has been rewarded an official status. The George Bush's war seems less violent from the viewpoint of an American Citizen while it looks more violent from a European viewpoint. And the act of war looks absolutely a terrorist act by the citizens of Iraq. Depending on who the reader is, the perception would be different while the action is the same: "One group of people attacking to kill another group of people." (One nation attacking another nation).

Nationalism seems to be racism for the lives of one group of people is valued more than the lives of another group of people. Bombing Polish by German in war was OK for German. Drone bombing Yemen and killing innocent Yemenites to eliminate a terrorist suspect by Saudi-States (Or bombing Syrians by Russia-Iran) is Ok too. While such actions in the Unites States would not be Ok. (The Drones kill even American citizens such as the 8-year-old American girl killed by the Drone in Yemen). The terrorist suspects inside the country are not bombed by Drones for the sake of injuring innocent citizens who are from "own nationality" or for having respect for own national law. However, terrorist suspects outside of the country are Drone bombed because there is no respect for the lives of such people because they are considered to be from "pagan nations" (As Bible refers to such nations). We bomb them because we don't have respect for international laws! Innocent women, men and children of nations suffer tremendously in the conflicts and wars created by such sick leaders. With push of a button, thousand could be killed. Nuclear wars could be started and the doom day could be near. The Sect leader, who believe in Armageddon and rest his hand swearing to the destruction of the World, will kill millions of people to execute justice with respect to the imaginary person of his God. The psychopathic leader thinks that he is the "Authority established by God" and he would use nuclear bombs at his disposal to make "the judgment day coming!"

Roman 13:1 *"Authorities are established by God."*

Bible: *"Judgment day and the Armageddon will happen by the hands of such Authority"*.

PRAISING CRIMINALS

In the United States, the Criminals are also respected as a hero! George Washington is praised as a hero regardless of him committing the Kidnapping or involuntarily servitude, which is: sex trafficking, child abuse, inflicting cruel and unusual punishment, discrimination, depriving persons of life and liberty without due process of law, denying persons the equal protection of the laws, violating the right of persons to be secured in their persons, effects and unreasonable seizures and denying the certain rights retained by people. He is a hero of independence even though he contained the independency of more than 300 men, women and children, and forced laboring them for the rest of their lives! He even sold their children into slavery. Washington purchased and traded the Kidnapped women, children and men and when they had run for freedom, he run $20 adds in newspaper and Kidnapped them back into slavery. Then, he punished them by flogging.

Respecting and praising the religion of Bible that supports crimes by the Government prompts officials and people to commit the crimes. People who are taught more than 4,000 years that it is OK to kill other men and take their woman and children as slave, would think of killing and Kidnapping as a norm and a culture. People don't see it as an act of crime because they have been taught at Temples and Churches that they are the chosen ones, who are sealed by God, and their God orders them to commit such crimes against certain people their God has made to be their enemy.

It becomes a norm to have others to do the hard work for free, or have others to do the hard work for a lesser fee…

Having Slaves and killing human in wars becomes a custom of pride. Killing, torturing and abusing others to gain from them becomes a norm. Abusing others to benefit own becomes a culture. Even the act of Genocide becomes a culture and normality. Kidnapping and fraud, indecency and mistreatment of others to benefit own interest becomes a habit for people and their leaders apply the same mentality harming other nations to benefit own. interests. That is why we hear a lot from politician saying: "It is in our national interests". The nation becomes selfish and ignorant. People would care less for each other and they would care less for other nations. They care less for environment. The society cares less for its own.

Officials and people who respect their leaders who committed a crime (A crime that was a norm to commit) or respect the discriminatory contents of a book, which commands to commit such crime, would also respect such discriminatory criminal actions of such book and their leaders. They are prompted to behave according to the racial preaching of the Bible or to follow their hero's discriminatory path. They follow the Bible's verses and they look up to their leaders and act against other races, genders or nations. They have been taught by the book and their heroes that: disrespecting, isolating, discriminating, abusing, torturing, Killing and Kidnapping of particular race, gender, nation and believer is OK. They would say: "If our Bible, our prophets and our leaders disrespected such race, so should we."

Bible Leviticus 26:44 *"You may acquire male and female slaves from pagan nations that are around you"*.

Bible Leviticus 26:45 *"They can be your position."*
Bible Leviticus 26:46 *"You may even bequeath them to your sons after you, to receive as possession; you can use them as permanent slaves. But in respect to your countrymen, the sons of Israel, you shall not rule with severity over on another."*
Ephesians 6:5 *"Slaves, be obedient to those who are your masters...with fear and trembling..."*
Matthew 26:30 *"Throw out the worthless slave into the outer darkness"*.
Titus 2:9 *"Urge the bond slaves to be subject to their masters in everything, to be well-pleasing, not argumentative, nor pilfering..."*
Colossians 4: *"Masters, grant to your slaves justice and fairness, knowing that you too have a Master in heaven"*.

Colossians 3:22 *"Slaves, in all things obey those who are your masters on earth… with sincerity of heart, fearing the Lord"*.

The ruling authority is taught to be having been established by God, chosen to be the superior race from the superior nation and it is OK to rule over other "pagan" nations with force, violence, torture and abuse and it is OK to kidnap the children of the "pagan" nations. The teaching of the book and raising statues of criminal leaders to praise them, promotes violence and racism that would invoke people and officials to behave violently, abusively and unjustly toward the "inferior" race mentioned in the Bible. (Police brutality toward African American, false punishments and imprisonment by Judges, Kidnapping Native American Children, Killing American 8-year-Old girl in Yemen with drone bomb, Kidnapping immigrant children such as this writer's child, shooting Gays at gay clubs, shooting African American at their churches, shooting Jewish at their synagogue, shooting Mexicans in Walmart or shooting Moslems at a Mosque in New Zealand). People are taught to be nationalists, patriotic and devoted Christians who would look up to their Bible and their leaders for guidance. Officials would look up to the crimes advertised in Bible as guidance and they would support the crime actions as well. They think of nations around Israel to be "pagan" and unworthy. They think of them being from another race (African, Middle Easterner or Latino), believing another religion (Idols or Islam), another gender (Gay or Lesbian) and they have been taught how to treat such persons for 2000 years by Bible and by the founder of the nation who was not in fond of the nation. (George Washington did not respect women and African, the majority of the population as part of the nation. Sound familiar?).

(Such preaching and teaching of such officials of the States have been punishing this writer who is an immigrant expressing himself and redressing his grievances against the authorities. The officials, who ignore the Kidnapping of immigrants' children committed by George Washington, ignored the Kidnapping of the child of this immigrant writer by a Washingtonian resident as well. The officials, who support the Kidnapping of immigrants' children confirmed in the Bible, supported the Kidnapping child of this immigrant writer too. The writer of this book has been punished by being separated from his child and not to see his child ever again!).

Recent foundlings of false imprisonments using DNA shows how many innocent people falsely imprisoned simply because two witnesses had lied to avenge against a race or person. Because the foundation of judiciary system is Bible based and testimony of two witnesses seem to be enough to punish the suspects:

Bible: Deuteronomy, 17:6: *"On the evidence of two witnesses or three witnesses, he who is to die shall be put to death; he shall not be put to death on the evidence of one witness"*.

Many high rank officials such as Presidents, Chief justices, Attorney Generals, Army Generals and Congressmen have committed the felony of the Kidnapping of immigrants (For 89 years) and discriminated against women and homosexuals for centuries but they never stand trial for their crimes saying that it was a norm to mistreat people in such ways. The reasoning is not a reasonable defense because the right to liberty was clearly mentioned in the

Constitution. Such criminal leaders committed the Kidnapping, tortured and abused millions of people because they followed the footsteps of their priests, prophets and leaders. They have been praising criminals who administered justice respecting the words of persons in Bible and respected the establishment of the religion within the Government.

The officials, officially believe and respect the violence and they apply the destruction in doing their official duty! Any officer of the law who is sworn into office by resting his hand on the Unconstitutional commands of the Bible in an official Oath ceremony, administers or legislates law with respect to persons, and any such officer who have respected a figure in a public office , who have committed a felony, endeavors the felony, and any such officer who have respected an establishment of religion within the Government, have committed Conspiracy to defraud the United States by defrauding the laws of the Constitution, and have committed Conspiracy against the United States by endeavoring and persuading crimes of violence against certain people of the United States. They have defrauded the United States laws of the Constitution by respecting person-al religious idealism to make policies that have harmed thousands of Americans, and they have respected the rich of persons over the poor in their law making policies or in their administering of justice that have harmed millions of American lives! 1,000 people, who die from hunger and cold each year, 700 soldiers, who were killed in wars each year for few years, 44,000 people, who are killed from suicide or homicide each year, is because the officials have personal respect for personal crimes! They believe and respect violence, death and destruction by swearing to the violent verses of their prophets! They have made a commitment to make crimes happen. By swearing their loyalty to the threats, they are making a commitment to commit the crimes not quitting them.

Such officials, who have a habit favoring persons of religion, also favor persons of rich by giving the rich persons the monopoly to run the Country's money supply. The rich pay to plan the elections and they are rewarded by favorable rules and regulations. The Treasury, along with Judiciary, Legislative and Executive, is person-alized as well. Private Banks are allowed to control the country's wealth by controlling the production of currency;

Conspiracy to have control of production of the Country' wealth. Persons and individuals (With assets) are given priority to have access to Treasury without being elected. Private persons control the public wealth by controlling the Country's Currency and Treasury through the Conspiracy of some officials who defrauded the United States laws. (1913, the Country was handed to individual persons to control the Country's Banking. The Federal Reserve is controlled by Private Banks. The most important branch of Government is personalized.) Officials, who have respects for religious person in their Oath, also have respects for persons of rich who have plenty of houses and rent them out. They ignore the 1,000 poor who die from hunger and cold who can't afford their rental prices. The statesmen have nullified their official Oath for respecting persons in their duty and for not performing their duty equally to the poor and to the rich. (In their official Oath they promise to treat rich and poor equal). Officials respect religious rich persons, and they ignore the poor with no religion. They make public policies personal and in favor of person-al religion and wealth, which harms the lives of million Americans who do not have religion or the wealth. By making commitment to the Bible and following a criminal hero, the statesmen have committed the Conspiracy to defraud the United States laws of the Constitution by respecting the persons of Paul and John and George, and they have committed themselves to commit crimes by following their prophets' and leader's commands to commit shooting, Kidnapping, torturing and discrimination toward millions. They have committed Conspiracy to Control the Currency, and they have committed Conspiracy to commit Genocide, and they have committed Conspiracy to defraud the United States, and they have committed Conspiracy to commit an offence against the United States by executing, legislating, and administering justice with respect to persons of religion and wealth. The Personal policy making of the officials, who have waged wars against immigrants and "pagan" nations, have caused the torture of American soldiers and civilians by hostile attacks in wars (Or friendly Drone bombs). They have caused nations to be the enemy of the States and they have provoked them to kill, Kidnap and torture American outside or inside the Country. Our dear persons in office, who have official interest in person-al interests, with their mono-policy of monopoly-ing the money of the nation, have person-al-ized and privatized the Control of the Currency of the Country. They have auctioned out the Control of money to the persons who have more money, shipped the work overseas, out working people, raised the housing prices, out homing people and once out-homed and out-worked people are in the streets in front of Towers and Banks, they are looked down by the owners of the Towers and Banks for not having home, work and savings! They are blamed for their own personal faults and personal decision making; that not having work, home and savings is the result of their own personal fault. That it is their own personal faulty decision making that caused them to suffer and not the fault of the officials who made the faulty, favorable, person-al decisions for the public!

The fault is the public's, not the republic's!

The public is blamed for not having home, work and insurance. The Republicans are not! The Republicans, who ship the work overseas and have raised the housing prices making it unaffordable, would not be blamed for the public lack of employment or housing.

Hundred thousands of the public suffer from wondering in the streets while Republicans have multiple housing and close their churches at nights to thousands of the public who shiver nights and days, pushed around, intimidated and injured by officers, many tortured, die or get killed, or live a miserable life designed by the Republicans who own Towers and Banks.

Such officials, the Republicans, Conspire to injure, oppress, make threats and intimidate people, and they have Kidnapped people's rights and forced them to live a miserable life in the streets. They commit Genocide by injuring hundreds of lives every day. And because they respect crimes and criminals by their ritual acts, and because the States committed the felony of Genocide at least for 89 years and toward Kidnapped African and the Natives (From 1776 to 1865), And because officials (Officially) believe in a religion that specifically intents to destroy a national, ethnic, racial, and religious group, therefore, such officials of the States have committed Genocide letting 1,000 people without home to die in the corner of the streets each year. (While they enjoy their comfort at their high buildings). They have committed Genocide because their Bible says:

"You shall strike all the men in the city with the edge of your sword. Only the women, the children, the animals, and all that is in the city, all its spoil, you shall take as booty for yourself. God gave them to you" (Deuteronomy, 20:13)

The officials transform the life of millions with the intend to destroy their race by causing them to die from hunger, cold, drug and violence or by preventing them from having family and offspring so their race would be wiped out. They force many to commit suicide and they cause many to lose mind wondering in the streets while addicted to drugs to ease their pain or selling their body to make a living. The officials did not quit committing the crimes they have had been committing for centuries but they affirm their commitments by swearing to their criminal book.

They make their commitment to the verses of the Bible in their Oath to commit the crimes!

They make commitment to act Bible like, Washington like. They have committed the crime act of Kidnapping for 89 years and they still separate children from their Native American parents or they still separate children from immigrants today. Such officials, who have interest in Bible

41

and wholly land, are addicted to commit crimes and they have shown their love for Kidnapping immigrants' children in such cases. They pray to the Bible that preaches to prey for such prey. It is an absolute Conspiracy. It is retaliation against the nation.

The State victimizes its own citizens and then prevents them from having access to justice or public facilities. And since the states contract out their sectors to privates, for example Transportation of schools to Bus Companies, or Banks, the victims in the streets are discriminated by such private companies as well.

Many people who become the victims in the streets would be denied employments or even using public facilities for not been dressed well, not having a home or transportation to apply for job. In addition, many States allow the private businesses to have the right to refuse services, which also limits the access to services for many victims in the street. The victims also are turned away from shelters, of which many force victims to attend religious ceremonies in order to be served. Also, if the victims report that their life is threatened they would not be protected. They are turned away from police stations and they are told that their life would be protected only if they had the money to pay for the protection! (Police officers would be provided to secure businesses with a fee but not for individuals with no money who are claiming that their life is in danger).

People in the streets are not respected because they are the people without property. They have never been part of the system to own men (Enslaving) or own any property. People who do not own property and are poor are considered property or subjects and they could be discarded if not needed:

"If a man pokes out the eye of his slave, he should be let go on the account of the lost eye".

(Exodus 21:26)

THE GENOCIDE

More than 30,000 innocent American citizens are killed each year by the Government policies that are devised by Corporations and Churches! The number is 10,000 times higher than the number of Americans who are killed by the ISIS in terrorist attacks inside the country in a single year! (3 Americans were killed in last year by the ISIS inside the country.)

Corporate Executives transfer the incomes of domestic workers to their own income when they transfer the domestic workers' jobs abroad. They pay foreign workers few dollars a day to do the job and what they save from paying them lesser than domestic works, they add it to their own one million dollar pay per day.

The outcome of this trans-action is that the income of the domestic workers becomes zero per day while their incomes mostly are transferred to the Corporate Executives' pay of one million dollars per day!

Corporations choose to exploit foreign workers rather than paying decent pay to domestic workers, who could disrupt their profits with their strikes for decent pay. So, after the Corporations transfer the jobs of the poor workers overseas, they have the Government evict them from their homes because the poor domestic workers would not be profitable any more as renters neither because their income have already been transferred to the income of the executives.

Corporate Executives, who become Government officials (Like Messrs. Mnuchin and Trump), are not concerned about the harm they inflict on poor workers, who wouldn't be profitable anymore, because they are raised to praise the selfish tradition of their Bible through their Churches that:

"Employers shouldn't be concerned about the harm they cause on their poor workers who aren't profitable anymore."
(Exodus 21:26)

The official culture of: "Inflicting harm on worker for the benefit of the employer." is derived from the ill ideology that has been preached for 2019 years:

"Employers could inflict harms on their poor workers for the sake of their own profit." *"Employers could beat their poor workers into submission."*
(Luke 12:47)

And poor workers aren't allowed to express their grievances against the employers:

"They have to be well pleasing and not be argumentive."
(Titus 2:9)
(That is why in 1980s in the U.S. they made it illegal for the workers to strike).

And if the poor workers are not profitable any more, they could just be discarded:

"If a master pokes the eye of his slave out, he should just let him go to live on his own."
(Exodus 21:26)

And if poor workers didn't comply, they could just be wasted:

46

"And if don't listen to judges and priests, they must be

stoned to death."

(Deuteronomy, 17:12)

Officials take their loyalty oath to the ill ideology which specifically describes in prints that: Believers in Bible with Capital, could exploit poor workers from neighboring countries, they could beat them into submission, and they could get rid of them when not profitable anymore.

They specifically are taught that: The poor workers are subjects that could be passed on as property:

"You can bequeath them to your children as inherited

property and can make them slaves for life, but you must

not rule over your fellow Israelites ruthlessly."

(Leviticus 25:46)

And the authorities, who think that they are established by God:

"Authorities are established by God."

(Roman 13)

Must follow every single biblical command:

"Neither an iota nor a dot is to be missed from the commands."

(Matthew, 5:18 Source: www.biblehub.com)

And if they don't follow the commands:

"If they don't obey and do not carry out the commands, the God of their Bible will make them blind and will make them to eat the flesh of their sons and daughters."

(Leviticus, 26:14-34)

Thus, the authorities are obligated to follow the commands and to get rid of the poor citizens who aren't profitable anymore. Besides, they are afraid to be punished by their God if they didn't comply. Their God has forced its authority over them and they ought to force their authority over poor workers! But since the public would not accept such a medieval act of Genocide to be committed right outright in the open, the Bible-ists get rid of useless poor workers following simple biblical guidelines:

1. By eliminating their food supply. The same way the Bible-ists settlers annihilated American Natives by eliminating their food supply of Bison, or the

English who eliminated the food supply of Indians by purchasing and hoarding most of their crops causing millions of them to die from starvation, or the Germans forcing Jews to live in ghettoes to die from malnutrition and starvation, the same way the Bible-ists authorities force the poor citizens into the streets to die from malnutrition and starvation. (More than 1,000 homeless die from hunger in America each year).

2. By restricting their living space. The same way they restricted the Native Americans living space into the sever cold weather of the North, or cramped Jews in Nazi camps to die from cold, starvation and diseases, the same way they restrict the living space of the homeless into the pavement of the streets to die from cold, starvation and diseases. (More than 1000 homeless die from cold in America each year).

3. By spreading virus, poison or drug among them. Exactly the same way they gassed Jews in gas

chambers, or spread viruses among Native Americans, or spread HIV viruses as vaccines among Africans in Africa or among gay community in America, or promoted the use of opium in East Asia, the same way they allow the spread of poisonous drugs among homeless population so they die from the use of poisonous drugs. (Each year more than 20,000 homeless die each year from drug use). (Bible-ists murdering with poison shouldn't considered a conspiracy theory since they did it to their own Bible-ists in WWI).

"Kill them with poison."
(Revelation 2:23)

4. By forcing them in desperation and depression so they commit suicide ending their own lives. Like the Kidnapped Africans who jumped overboard into the sea to ease their pain and fear, or Jews who committed suicide to end their suffering in concentration camps, the homeless commit suicide

from desperation and depression. (Over 28,000 homeless committed suicide in 2017).

5. Creating violence, conflict and unsafe environment for them so they are forced to commit offences to survive which cause them to eliminate their own population through violence or getting arrested, prosecuted and executed. (Thousands of homeless are killed in the street, shot dead by police, or prosecuted each year or even executed).

The poor workers are evicted into the streets to die from cold, hunger, use of drugs and violence and they are forced into depression to commit suicide or they are forced into desperation to commit homicide. They are pushed to live in a violence environment that leaves them no other choice but to commit offence to stay alive. (Like selling their body or selling drugs). Just like the authority itself that claims that it is left with no other choice but to act violently and commit the offence of shootings and drone bombings of others to defend itself from possible threats, many abused citizens are left with no other choice but to act violently and commit offence to defend themselves from <u>the clear authoritarian threats</u>!

Just like George Washington who left with no other choice but to act violently and committed offence shooting his superior officers to have access to more land and to force labor more poor workers on his land (In the form of slavery), many abused citizens are left with no choice but to join gangs to have access to more land and exploit more human (In the form of sex slavery).

If a rich authority commits the offence, he will become hero and his praised for his actions but if poor citizens commit the offences they are gangs, criminals and terrorists!

The poor is abused by the authority for so long that they join together shaping gangs or mafia to compete with the abusive corrupt authority in stealing wealth through mischief. (Many even choose to join terrorist groups abroad to fight injustice).

The ideology that encourages violence, racism and terrorism, creates more of the violence, racism and terrorism.

So many times in the past, the Bible-ists have proven to be committed to their ill criminal ideology and they have committed Genocide to eliminate the poor people they hated so much by: Burning spiritual teenage girls alive in the fire, Kidnapping Africans into Slavery, gassing million Jews in gas chambers, or even poisoning their own members! (Like Jimmy Jones who murdered more than 900 of their own group).

Therefore, claiming that the Bible-ists currently committing the Genocide that is in progress shouldn't be considered a conspiracy theory because the suspects had motives for committing the crimes, which are clearly printed in their ideological book of Bible, and they have committed the Genocide so many times in the past.

The Bible-ists clergy men, who made money by preaching, had to eliminate their competitors of magicians, spirituals and gypsies who stole their customers. Thus, they inflicted fear among people with the illusionary characters of Devil or Satan as the enemy of God that could enter in human making them ill or causing them to commit sins. (Perhaps of their lack of knowledge of germs and bacteria, they called the cause of illness bad spirit or evil). And they convinced people that the Satan enters into the gypsies and homeless people who spread the bad spirit and that's why God make such people homeless, and mentally disabled as their punishment.

So, gypsies, spirituals and mentally ill people, who were homeless and wondering in towns, committed sins by spreading the bad spirits. (And perhaps they might have spread diseases for they traveled). And they ought to be punished and be eliminated for acting against God. In this way, the clergymen eliminated their liberal competitors who had harmed their income. (Mostly burnt them alive for believing that the bad spirit would only be eliminated by fire).

The same way today, the Bible-ists clergy men hate liberals who would harm their profits. (Such as atheism that spreads among young people who don't attend nor contribute to churches or socialism that forces churches to pay taxes and spreads among poor workers).

This superstitious slander to hate such poor people is taught through religious communities supported by Churches and Bible, which is praised by officials in public offices as well, and the public opinion has turned against poor workers, who become homeless, drug addicts, prostitutes or mentally ill.

(I have heard repeatedly by the boyfriend of the prime Kidnapper in the case, Mr. J., that I shouldn't have had helped her daughter, the mother of my child, because she was evil and made mentally disabled by God to suffer! That made me so eager to help and save people like her, who are suffering so many similar abuses from their families, Churches, Government and Corporations. Specially knowing that historically such poor people have been thrown in the fire alive to be burnt because they were thought of having Satan in them and the only way to get rid of the Satan was by fire! –perhaps because fire killed the germs and healed wounds).

By evicting the poor people into the streets, the officials put the burden on city people, who are already made to think that the existence of such people harms their community; Poor people, who wonder around, carry Satan, germs and viruses therefore their death or suffering are not important for the public. (I have heard repeatedly that if they fall from the cliff no one cares! And I have seen hunters who hunt them in the cities and the officials do not investigate the crimes because their disappearances are not important and it even lifts the burden to deal with them! That is why no one is aware of the Genocide in progress).

Churches, Corporations and Government, who have their hands on the Bible in public office, treat poor workers, who will become homeless or mentally disabled wondering in the streets, as sick souls carrying Satan who ought to be eliminated or they are subjects and the waste of the economy that ought to be discarded. And that is why thousands of homeless, who do not profit the economy that is designed to benefit the tiny group in charge of Churches, Corporations and Government, are left to die in the streets and such a criminal action goes unnoticed because the public opinion is turned against such a waste, lazy sinners who carry devil and germ around. (The same way they turned the public opinion against teenage spirituals as witches, the slaves, Natives, the mentally disabled, gypsies and the Jews so they could be gassed, burned alive in the fire, or whipped and murdered).

Thus, the final solution to eliminate the waste of the economy is done systematically by the collaboration between Churches, Corporations and the Government:

1. Churches, which close their doors at 9.p.m to homeless, consider them sinners who carry Satan who ought to be harmed and:

2. Corporations and the Government promote Church's ideology in public office and evict poor workers from their jobs and homes into the streets to suffer and die.

The authorities have religious justification for their criminal actions because it is their religious duty and obligation to eliminate the evil and the Satan who appears in human! Just like the ISISts, who believe that they will be rewarded by their God for murdering the Satanic Americans, the Bible-ists believe that they would be rewarded by eliminating the Satanic Americans!

Just like the Islamist terrorist clergymen, who control illiterate, racist, conservative people with superstition and psychopathy in attacking none believer liberals to keep their power status and obtain money from people, the priests and pastors control illiterate, racist, conservative people with superstition, illusions and psychopathy in attacking none believer liberals to keep their power status and obtain money from people.

The Government, Churches and Corporations use their Bible and Capital in setting abusive policies that only benefits the high rank officials while such policies cause economic hardship on poor families which result in more conflicts among family members that causes thousands of women and children being abused in the family violence and conflicts by the family members who are distressed, religiously unsecured and weakened economically. The economic hardship causes more abuses when it forces families to break apart by divorce or when parents would face court orders and are separated from their children.

Government officials cause economic hardship on mostly poor families, they create instability and violence, and their mischief allow the drug abuse by the family members which cause even more family separation, abuses, violence and crimes.

Then, the Government that is the main cause of the conflicts, abuses, violence and separations of families, steps in to be the judge of the conflicts, abuses, and violence and they separate families from their children to protect them from conflicts, abuse, and the violence that they have created?!

Churches and Corporations have funded the corrupted Government officials to create the economic hardship, conflicts, abuses and violence, then they step in helping the Government in mentoring or treating the problem they have helped to create!?

For their support of their picked officials, Churches and Corporations are rewarded contracts, Tax deductions, subsidies, bail outs and cash credits, and they receive favorable regulations to obtain money, property, and to have access to women and children! (Thousands of priests sexually have abused children and hundreds of Corporate executives sexually abused women using their status and money).

And the Government officials return Churches and Corporations favors by promoting their abusive and unconstitutional ideologies in public offices and by promoting their abusive economic policies for the public that enables all of them to obtain status of power over children and women, who are abused by the promotion of such abusive religious and economic ideologies.

The Bible, that is mostly represented by men who are in charge of Churches and Corporation and have formed a conservative Government, weakens the status of woman in society by requiring women to be quiet and be submissive to their husbands:

"Wives, be subject to your husbands, as is fitting in the lord."

(Colossian 3)

Their children are named after their husbands, they are prosecuted for showing their nipples in public and the promotion of Bible and Church helps electing more men with Capital in office than women who are weakened economically for being banned from office for 1920 years. (Men earn more by preaching and wedding in Churches and they earn more through their saving assets that were saved by abusing poor workers and slaves for centuries and prohibiting women from earning for thousands of years. The disadvantage of the promoting the Bible in society for women could easily be viewed in the appointment of judges in the 8th appeal court district, for example, that out of 9 judges appointed, 8 are male and only one judge is a female. Or the U.S. never having a woman as a president in the last 244 years, or the country currency having pictures of mostly men is a proof of the disadvantages of the sexist and racist teachings of the Bible).

Bible and Church give advantage to religious men to earn Capital by working, preaching as a priest and earn to wed and to fool the public to gain their trust to abuse their children, while the Bible and Church forces women into prostitution to please the men who are under the cover of priesthood!

The fact that for 244 years the U.S. never had a woman as president, or having a picture of a child abuser man on the currency (Washington) instead of mother Teresa for example, are the examples of how the promotion of the Bible in the public office benefits the men more than women in reaching to the Capitol to earn more Capital!

(Priests are allowed to serve in army as chaplains but LGBTs are not! Bible says that LGBTs must be stoned to death).

The economically weakened mothers, who are made unsecured religiously when they are put down and treated as second citizens along with minorities, are evicted from their jobs and homes into the streets and they would be forced to feed their children by selling their body to the men who control the Church and the State. Women workers, who can't follow the jobs that are shipped to China and can't pay the high cost of housing, or the mothers whose children are separated from them unjustly, would be evicted from their home into homelessness and they are forced into prostitution to be abused by men who control the Church, Banking, politics and businesses, whose executives prefer to pay an Indian worker $8 per day rather than paying American woman worker $80 per day and the amount they save from paying lower wages to foreign workers will be added to the executives' own pay of $1 million per day! Such policy cuts the pay of thousands of American women workers to $0 per day, when their job is transferred to India, and they will be evicted from their home by the Government for not being able to pay the high rents to the landlords, who are the Executives who have invested their one million dollar pay per day in lucrative apartment building and real estate businesses for more profit!

The Government with collaboration with Corporations and Churches use their Bible and their Capital to have power over people whom they have unsecured in the society by their Bible and their Capital: children, women, the poor, minorities and LGBTs. You put the dots together and don't miss any iota:

The President of the Government, that criminalizes women entertainers, who please men for money, pays to women entertainers to please himself and pays her to shut her up!

And the priests, who hear the confessions of child abusers and sinners, become sinners and child abusers who are allowed to continue their work!

The Government that makes threats to harm LGBTs, and praises the priests, bans LGBTs from Army but allows Priests to serve as Chaplains!

And bank executives, who own many homes, are given billions of dollars loan by Government officials while people without home are given nothing, their jobs are given to foreigners and they are left to die in the corner of the streets!

The Government, Churches and Corporations that are the threat to families, women and children, pretend that they care for them when they separate parents from their children and treat them with painful drugs in their private mental health facilities or when they encourage them to read the Bible and receive Church services to be made safe around women and children!

The officials, who have created an unsafe republic for the public and publicly making threats to harm the public and set abusive policies that has harmed the public, police the public for safety!

Officials, pastors and executives insecure people by promoting a violent ideology, setting destructive economic policies that primarily are based on selling more of murdering tools of weapons and guns, exporting jobs overseas and raising the cost of housing, then they police the insecurities that they have created just to secure their own securities!

The Government, Churches, Banks and Weapon manufacturers support terrorism by supporting Kidnapping and Kidnappers that are printed on their papers of Bible and their paper bills (Washington who abused children in the form of slavery), commit terrorism by recruiting Police and Army to secure their assets!

(The Police who shoot people in the back and the terrorists who shot dead 49 people in gay club, shot 11 African American in church, shot 9 Jewish in synagogue recently, are terrorists who are recruited, schooled, and funded by Government chaplains, Church pastors and Corporation executives to commit such crimes to protect their Bible ideology and to secure their abusive economic policies).

Creating violence and crimes and destabilizing communities and nations is another of their money making scheme so their companies could sell more guns and security equipment, medical supplies or benefit from private mental and correctional facilities.

How an economic policy that is designed to benefit less than one percent of the population by increasing the price of housing, exporting jobs, creating violence and crimes and destabilizing communities and nations, could benefit the public that is used and abused as a money making tool for the one percent group in charge of the economy?

How an economy that is designed to create waste to increase demands in order to grow the economy for a few people, could guarantee that it would not waste people to grow their economy specially when their ideology clearly mentions in prints that they could abuse or waste poor people to benefit from them economically!?

What is the guarantee that such a tiny group of people, who have designed an economy that benefits their own tiny group of people and would make more money from insecurity, conflict and wars and by detaining more people in their private facilities, selling more guns and weapons and security equipment in conflicts and wars, would be willing to create safety for the public if such a safety lowers their profits?

If they make money out of wars, why should they keep peace?

If they make money out of violence, conflict and insecurity, why should they create safety and security?

What is the guarantee that Private Bankers and weapon manufacturers, who have harmed the public only to benefit from the increase in housing prices and the jobs being shipped overseas, would not intentionally create conflicts and wars inside the country and abroad if they benefit trillions of dollars from weapons and loans that will be sold in more wars and conflicts?

THE CLOWNS IN THE GOWNS

Judges angered by this writer for revealing their crimes took revenge against him claiming that he is crazy and they Kidnapped his child away from him and sent him to mental hospital to mute him and his claim. Below is the copy of this writer's claim which was blocked by the Conspiracy of the Judges who blocked the claim from proceeding to prevent their own crimes from being revealed to the public:

NO. _____

_____

IN THE

SUPREME COURT OF THE UNITED STATES

<u>M. K.</u>   PETITIONER

VS.

9th Cir. Case No: 17-35730

MOTION FOR EXTENSION OF TIME FOR FILING A WRIT OF

CERTIORARI

(EXTRAORDINARY CONDITION)

To: Honorable Justice Ruth Ginsburg

---

*"KIDNAP THE CHILDREN OF THE PAGAN PEOPLE
AROUND YOU."*
"GOD HAS GIVEN THEM TO YOU."
(Bible, Deuteronomy, 20:14. Leviticus, 25:44. Source:

www.biblehub.com)

Many officials of the state have committed themselves to

the Kidnapping threats made toward millions of Americans

when they swear their loyalty to the Bible to take office.

By their actions, they have conspired to injure, oppress, and threatened to Kidnap children!

18 U.S. Code 241: "If two or more persons conspire to injure, oppress, threaten... attempt to Kidnap...may be sentenced to death."

And the officials who have conspired to injure people cannot be immune from prosecution because:

Title 18, 373 (c) "It is not a defense to a prosecution under this section that the person solicited could not be convicted of the crime because he lacked the state of mind required for its commission, because he was incompetent or irresponsible, or because he is immune from prosecution or is not subject to prosecution."

The biblical commands of their Bible considered Godly cannot be censored and the officials, who rest their hand on the written threats, must fulfill them:

"Everything that is written in the Bible must be fulfilled. Neither an iota nor a dot is to be missed from the commands."

(Matthew, 5:18 Source: www.biblehub.com)

The state officials, who are sworn in by the threats that are made toward "pagan" people, had to harm the "pagan" parent in the case because if they had not obeyed and did not carry out the commands:

"If they don't obey and do not carry out the commands, the God of their Bible will make them blind and will make them to eat the flesh of their sons and daughters."

(Leviticus, 26:14-34)

Such authorities believe that they are established by God:

"Authorities are established by God."

(Roman 13)

And their belief tells them to beat the people, whom they Kidnap, into submission:

"Beat the people you Kidnap in submission."

71

And their belief tells them to crush those who believe otherwise:

"Crush those who believe otherwise by stone." ("All who do not seek the LORD, the God of Israel, must be put to death.") (2Chronicles 15:13)

And they must forbid those, whom they have Kidnapped and crushed, from entering into their house of authority:

"Those whose testicles are crushed cannot enter the house of God."

(Deuteronomy, 23:1)

And judges must torture and mute those who argue and do not listen to them:

"They have to be well pleasing and not be argumentive."
"And if don't listen to judges and priests, they must be stoned to death."

(Titus 2:9, Deuteronomy, 17:12)

And people who believe in anything other than their Bible:

"Those who do not seek the Lord of Israel must be stoned to death, be given poison, their little ones be dashed in pieces, their pregnant women be ripped open, their children burnt, slaughtered, Kidnapped, their homes burnt down, and their skirts be lifted so others could see their nakedness".! (2Chronicles 15:13. Hosea 13:16. Amos 1:7, 8. Ezekiel 9:6. Deuteronomy 20:13, 14. Micah 1:6. Nahum 3:5, 15. Source: www.biblehub.com. Revelation 2:23. Source: New American Standard Bible, Lockman Foundation.)

The dad in the case was treated exactly the same way as he was supposed to be treated: his child Kidnapped, he was crushed and was not allowed in the court house, he forced to take drugs to be tortured and be muted, and his arguments were dismissed for questioning the authorities.

The Government threatens to Kidnap the children of "pagan" dads from nations around Israel, and it threatens to crush none believer dads who question the authority and judges who are established by God, then it applies the threats to the dad in the case, who is from nations around Israel, a none believer, and who questioned the authority and judges whom he believes are established by people like him to protect him not making threats to kill him!

The Government that has a history of Kidnapping the children of nationals around Israel (For 89 years from 1776- 1865), and the Government that separated Native children to be raised by their "own" Bible-ists people, did separated the baby from the Native dad in the case to be raised by Bible-ists. (He is a Native of Earth from Persia and has been around for 7,000 years).

The Government that respects the Bible that says:

> *"Kill their men and take their children."*
> (Deuteronomy, 20:13)

Will copy what the Bible says: *"Kill the Indian. Save the man"* (U.S. Captain Richard. H. Brat).

The Bible-ists believing in the Kidnapping that is commanded in their Bible, or believing in George Washington, who committed the Kidnapping, contradicts with the belief of the dad in his own gene, which abolished the Kidnapping and released the same Bible-ists from captivity 2,500 years ago! The dad's gene of Cyrus the Great released Jewish from captivity and built their temple in Israel. They were not released from captivity then, to Kidnap his gene Prince today! (They have to forget the past and not to try to take revenge from those who kept them in captivity thousand years ago. Because they could wrongfully Kidnap their own Prince or Son of their Lord! The Persian King is considered Lord in Bible and his gene Prince is Son of their Lord. Had they read their own Bible, they would not have Kidnapped their own Prince; the Son of their Lord!)

The Government, that has a history of Kidnapping people from around Israel into slavery and separating their children from them, still makes threats towards nationals around Israel in its official ceremonies and it does (still!) separate the children from such parents! (The children of Latin immigrants and thousands of other citizens like the dad in the case).

The Religious Government that has a habit of torturing and executing indigenous and ingenious people (Natives, Africans, Socrates, Galileo, Jesus) and burning scientists, writers and teenage girls alive in the fire for ridiculing their religious foundation, still tortures indigenous and ingenious writers who ridicule their religious foundation; like the dad in the case. The Government that is supposed to behave maliciously toward the dad and take his baby a way, to beat him and drug him, to torture and mute his arguments, did to him the malicious things it meant to do and dismissed his claim as malicious to mute his argument!

"They have to be well pleasing and not to be argumentive and if they don't listen to priests or judges, they must be stoned to death."!

(Titus 2:9. Deuteronomy, 17:12)

And they dismissed his case because they couldn't have allowed his claim to proceed because he wasn't supposed to question the authority and judges in the first place. (The same way they arrested Julian Assange for revealing their crimes). Thus, they prevented the parent from expressing his grievances against the state by psychologically torturing him taking his child away and by forcing him to take drugs that caused extreme psychological pain and trauma on him, detaining him, intimidating him by arrests, warrants and false felony charges, dismissing his case and blocking him from entering the court house that prevented him from filing his motions of grievances properly and on a timely manner.

Separating children from parents is a cruel and unusual punishment that causes pain, severe depression, loss of memory, loss of concentration, sleeplessness, emotional instability, anger, anxiety, trauma, cognitive disability, panics, heart attack, prolonging thought process, coma and stroke which could cause brain injury or death. The pain and confusion in mind distracts the brain from sending timely signals to the heart which could cause a heart attack or it could unbalance the blood pressure in the vessels of the brain causing, stroke, brain injury, coma or prolonging the though process. It is also possible that the victim, who is suffering from severe depression caused by the separation, commit suicide.

Taking a child from a parent takes so much out of the parent. It takes the life out of the family. The injury does not take the blood away from the body instantly, but it takes the thought process away right away. It is not murder, but it is worse than a murder! The injury does not inflict the body primarily. The injury inflicts the mind. The victim is not injured to bleed to death, but is left to be tortured psychologically and lose mind enough to commit suicide.

The injury does not cut the blood vein...
The injury causes one to go insane!

The sever mind issue will damage the brain tissue prolonging the thought process preventing the parent from completing easy tasks properly or on a timely manner, which along with court distractions, litigations, warrants, arrests and detentions, and the missing days from work to do the lawyering (Washington State does not provide defense attorney in family cases), causes the parents to lose work.

Moreover, the parent would be defamed in the view of employers, renters and friends who would think that he must have done something seriously wrong that his child is taken away from him by the orders of the court and they don't trust him anymore to offer him job, home or friendship. Thus:

1) The Parent whose baby is evicted from his life is a dead person walking who can't keep a job and will be evicted from home and forced into homelessness and:

2) He is also deterred by community, employers, friends, and court and he could not earn income to pay for meal, paper, printing papers, or transportation to get to courts to file on time (Once he made it to the court but didn't have 15 cents to print a paper, so he wrote his motion on a toilet paper. It is recorded) and:

3) He goes hungry, shivering in cold in the rain outside, his belonging and ID would be stolen and he will not have a certain address to receive court orders by mail on time and:

4) He will not be allowed into Federal Court House for not having an ID to file court orders properly and on a timely manner and:

5) His car will be towed for not paying the tab, his driver license will be suspended for not paying tickets, and he could not receive the suspension notification for not having a certain address and:

6) He is arrested with the felony charge of driving with a suspended license while his car is towed and:

7) When he accidently meets his child in a park, he is wrongfully accused of stocking and the felony of violating the restraining order but he could not be

notified of the charges that was set for a hearing for show cause by mail for not having an address and:

8) He is issued warrant of arrest for not showing up at court which prevented him from entering federal building to file on time and when he does enters the court:

9) He gets arrested and sent to jail and:

10) When he performs a protest in front of the court house, the officials view him as a screaming homeless man who shouldn't be allowed into the federal building ever again which also causes:

11) The officials to detain him in the excuse of mental treatment over a month without giving him the access to due process of law to file on time and:

12) Causing the officials to mute him and torture him by giving him extremely painful drugs. He is judged to be malicious and if he is not one, he is made into one! Whatever takes to shut him up from speaking against priests, authorities and judges will do. None believers, Entertainers and dancers who talk to their own God are judged as mentally ill who are to be executed, burnt alive in the fire or stoned to death:

"Men without testicles are not welcome to the house of God." "Sorcerer and spirituals shall be stoned to death." "Women must be quiet."

(Exodus 22:18. And: 1Timothy 2:12, Deuteronomy 23:1)

All of the above delayed or prevented the filing on time for the petition for the writ of a certiorari by dad who could not have finished the easy task of certifying his mail due to the prolonging of his thought process and lacking funds which he has been suffering from since his baby was Kidnapped from his arms 4 years ago by the Arm forces.

(The Plaintiff mailed his petition for the writ of the certiorari on time many times but the court discarded the mails! He had sent many mails within 90 days and he had called many times to check on their status but the court claimed they didn't receive the mails while U.P.S. confirmed that they delivered the mails! It seems that some officials do not wish to hear the bitter truth that is against their belief and they must have discarded the mails.)

What it took me few minutes to write 4 years ago will take me a week to write! (It took me one week to prepare one page of these papers).

I hope the court takes in consideration the above factors in my request for the time extension for my petition for a writ of certiorari.

The official motive was to crush the dad with trauma,
Hush him with drugs, time out and coma.
With such commotion,
How could a dad have a proper motion?!

Respectfully submitted,

M. K.

Date

NO. _____

_____

IN THE

SUPREME COURT OF THE UNITED STATES

M. K.   PETITIONER

VS.

U.S.A.   RESPONDENT(S)

ON PETITION FOR A WRIT OF CERTIORARI TO

9th CIRCUIT COURT OF APPEALS. Case No: 17-35730

PETITION FOR A WRIT OF CERTIORARI

QUESTIONS REPRESENTED

a) How officers, who take their oath to the threats made toward public in their Bible, could protect the public from such threats?!

b) How could an African American officer of the law, the honorable justice Clarence Thomas, be protective of African Americans if he is sworn into office by the statutes that command the beating of the African Americans?! (*"Beat the African Americans in submission"*. Luke 12:47)

c) How could a woman justice, the honorable justice Sonya Sotomayor, be protective of woman's rights if she is sworn into office by the statutes that prohibit women from becoming a justice?! (*"Women must be quiet. They cannot take authority over men"*. 1Timothy 2:12).

d) How could people be safe from the President, Senators, Judges and Police officers who are sworn into office to harm them?!

e) How could the Washington State judges, who work under the flag of a child abuser: George Washington, preside over child abuse matters?

(George Washington committed Kidnapping or involuntarily servitude that is: sex trafficking, child abuse, inflicting cruel and unusual punishment, discrimination, depriving persons of life and liberty without due process of law, denying persons the equal protection of the laws, violating the right of persons to be secured in their persons, effects and unreasonable seizures and denying the certain rights retained by people).

f) How could Washington State judges:

1. Who respect a child abuser as their hero and:

2. Who respect unconstitutional statutes of the Bible and:

3. Who respect the Kidnapping threats and the prejudice statutes made in their Bible towards the dad in the case,

have made their judgments
without prejudice toward the
dad?

g) What reasons caused a judge to restrain the dad
from visiting his baby permanently?!

h) Could judges, who respect prejudice statutes and
prejudice commander, command their judgments
without prejudice?!

i) Why dad's request of removing such malicious
threats made toward public, in public offices, and
by public officers is considered a malicious claim?

j) Did appeal court ever read the dad's argument that
the Title 18, 373(c) would remove the immunity
clause from the Title 28 1915 A (b) (1) (2)? Meaning
that the officials who are accused of committing
Conspiracy and Defrauding the United States will
not be immune from prosecution and the case
should not have been dismissed as frivolous or
malicious.

k) While the Federal courts referred to the Title 28 1915 A (b) (1) (2) in dismissing the case as malicious or frivolous, shouldn't they have applied the section (b) of the same Title, that allow part of the claim to be reviewed? (In order to protect the child and public from possible harms).

    A. To protect the child from:

        1. The Kidnapping that was in process. And:

        2. To protect him from further injuries since the Kidnappers have already had cut him and killed his puppy!

    B. To protect the public from:

        3. Being separated from their children by officers who have their hands on the threats that are made towards them. And:

        4. To prevent injuries that could result from unjust separations of

the children from their parents by such officers, which could even cause the children to die? (For example the 7, or 8 years old Guatemalan children who died while at the Government custody). And:

5. To prevent children, women, Homosexuals, Africans, Latinos, Asians, Arabs and many nationals around Israel of being harmed by the officials who have their hands on the threats that are made towards such group of people!

I) Why the courts ignored the child abuses in process?

1. The Kidnapping of the child in process

2. The 2" injury cut caused on him by the Kidnappers

m) Why the courts ignored the Perjury committed by the Prime Kidnapper at the Trial? (It is recorded her saying that she didn't know about the cut. The injury is clearly showing in the picture that presented to the court).

n) Why Federal courts ignored the unconstitutional actions of the state court, which:

    1. Forced the dad to take an Oath instead of affirmation and:

    2. Forced him to raise his religious right hand to take the Oath. (Shouldn't he be allowed to take affirmation to tell the truth without lifting any body parts?).

o) Didn't WA State have a conflict of interests with the dad at the time of Trial for:

    1. The dad filing a suit against the WA State that was proceeding in the same time in federal court by the order of a magistrate.

2. The State could have protected own name in the case because the naming the State after a child abuser was in the conflict between a Government entity and the individual(s).

3. WA State judges working under the flag of a child abuser (George Washington) who abused the same group of dads by separating their children from them (Mr. Washington Kidnapped immigrant children from nations around Israel because his Bible commands it. The dad in the case is also an immigrant from nations around Israel) And:

4. The judges rested their hands on the threats that were made toward the same group of dads (They had sworn their loyalty to the crimes! Bible commands that

nationals around Israel are to be harmed and their children are to be separated from them).

p) Shouldn't Federal court have approved the dad's motion of Stay for WA State having a conflict of interests?

q) Why the State court ignored the documents below in their decision making:

1. That the dad had signed up his baby boy in Ballet class and:

2. He proved to be a feminist writer who insisted that his child keep his mother's last name so women equal rights could be promoted and:

3. He had been evaluated by the court appointed psychologist of being above the average intelligence and:

4. The fact that he worked, paid Taxes for at least 6 years, had home and a car and raised his child for 6 years and:

5. That he worked as a real Father outside of Church system helping endangered victims who were left to be rotten in the street by the religious system and:

6. That he has been sacrificing so much of his lifetime caring for one of such victims, the mother of his child, for 8 years voluntarily taking her to vacation to Italy and Australia!

r) And why dad viewed as a crazy person who abandoned his child who deserved to be restrained from seeing his child permanently?

s) How could a dad, who signed up his baby boy for ballet lessons, have abandoned his child?!

t) Could we conclude that the judges who ruled against the dad:

1. Disliked him, got mad at him and discriminated against him for questioning their belief and:

2. They took revenge by punishing him for questioning their abusive hero and:

3. They considered him an inferior "pagan" person who was not supposed to complain about the authority that is stablished by God. And:

4. They dismissed his case so their own malicious threats towards public could not be revealed And:

5. They conspired against him by wrongfully claiming that he is an abusive and malicious dad who needs to be detained, given strong medicine to be muted

and made harmless for public and:

6. They abused laws to obscure injustice and obstruct justice by ignoring his motions, reasoning and grievances and dismissing his claims as frivolous and malicious so their conspiracies and obstruction of justice seemed legal. And:

7. They committed the same exact conspiracy crimes that the prime Kidnappers committed: they wrongfully accused the dad of child abuse and ruined his life to cover up their own abusive actions and in process they helped the Kidnapping of his child. (The prime Kidnapper committed custodian interference and they had abused the child by cutting him and they accused the Father

wrongfully of child abuse to cover up their own criminal actions). And:

u) Could we conclude that in the same way many Police officers, judges, senators and presidents could have committed conspiracy crimes to harm certain group of people intentionally because they are raised to praise their own ideology that commands them to harm such groups of people?

v) And could we conclude that the Kidnapping of African Americans from 1776 till 1865 and numerous other crimes would not have happened if officials had not respected a religious establishment that commands to its followers to commit the Kidnapping and other crimes? ("Take slaves from nations around you and you could beat them to submission." Leviticus 25:44 and Luke 12:47)

w) And could we conclude that the Kidnapping of the baby from his dad would not have happened if the officials had not committed themselves to the crimes and the criminals?

x) And since making threats would result in violence and crimes, isn't reasonable to allow this claim to proceed so that the United States could not be Defrauded further by threats, violence, crimes, hatred and racism that are promoted by high rank officials?

y) Also, why the Federal court ignored the 26 pages of accusations of Conspiracy and Defrauding the United States against many other officials from other branches of Government?

z) Wouldn't a promise to administer justice WITH respect to persons of John, Paul and George right in an oath, nullify the oath of office and void the judgments of judges who never became official? How could judges administer justice with respect to constitutional and unconstitutional commands simultaneously?

CONSTITUTIONAL AND STATUARY PROVISIONS INVOLVED

STATUTES THAT SUPPORT THE CLAIM:

(1) CONSPIRACY

Title 18, 371, (a), and Title 18, 373 (c): *"It is not a defense to a prosecution under this section that the person solicited could not be convicted of the crime because he lacked the state of mind required for its commission, because he was incompetent or irresponsible, or because he is immune from prosecution or is not subject to prosecution"*.

Title 18, 2384: *"If two or more persons conspire...by force to prevent, hinder, or delay the execution of any law of the United States...they shall each be fined under this title or imprisoned not more than twenty years, or both."*

(2) CONSPIRACY AND TORTURE:

Title 18 U.S. Code, 2340A(c) *"A person who conspires to commit an offense under this section shall be subject to the same penalties (other than the penalty of death) as the penalties prescribed for the offense, the commission of which was the object of the conspiracy."*

(3) CONSPIRACY AGAINST RIGHTS

Title 18 U.S. Code, 241: *"If two or more persons conspire to injure, oppress, threaten, or intimidate any person in any*

State... <u>*or if such acts include kidnapping or an attempt to*</u> <u>*kidnap, aggravated sexual abuse*</u> *or an attempt to commit aggravated sexual abuse, or an attempt to kill, they shall be fined under this title or imprisoned for any term of years or for life, or both, or may be sentenced to death."*

(4) GENOCIE

Title 18 U.S. Code, 1091: *"Whoever, whether in time of peace or in time of war and with the specific intent to destroy, in whole or in substantial part, a national, ethnic, racial, or religious group as such— imposes measures intended to prevent births within the group; or transfers by force children of the group to another group".* *"A fine of not more than $1,000,000 or imprisonment for not more than twenty years, or both, in any other case."*

(5) ENTICEMENT INTO SLAVERY AND INVOLUNTARY SERVITUDE:

Title 18 U.S. Code, 1583 (a)(1): *"Whoever kidnaps or carries away any other person, with the intent that such other person be sold into involuntary servitude, or held as a slave; shall be fined under this title, imprisoned not more than 20 years, or both."*

Also Title 18 U.S. Code, 1584 (a)

(6) KIDNAPPING

Title 18 U.S. Code, 1201: *"Whoever unlawfully seizes, confines, inveigles, decoys, kidnaps, abducts, or carries away and holds for ransom or reward or otherwise any person...shall be punished by imprisonment for any term of years or for life..."*

(7) FAILURE TO REPORT CHILD ABUSE:

Title 18 U.S. Code, 2258,*"A person who, while engaged in a professional capacity or activity described in subsection (b) of section 226 of the Victims of Child Abuse Act of 1990 on Federal land or in a federally operated (or contracted) facility, learns of facts that give reason to suspect that a child has suffered an incident of child abuse, as defined in subsection (c) of that section, and <u>fails to make a timely report</u> as required by subsection (a) of that section, shall be fined under this title or imprisoned not more than 1 year or both."*

(8) OBSTRUCTION OF CRIMINAL INVESTIGATIONS

Title 18 U.S. Code, 1510 (a): *"Whoever willfully endeavors by means of bribery to obstruct, delay, or prevent the communication of information relating to a violation of any criminal statute of the United States by any person to a criminal investigator shall be fined under this title, or imprisoned not more than five years, or both.*

(9) *OBSTRUCTION OF JUSTICE:*

Title 18 U.S. Code, 1505, 1506, 1512 (a) (B), 1512 (a) (2) (A), and 1519.

Title 18 U.S. Code, 1512 (k*): "Whoever conspires to commit any offense under this section shall be subject to the same penalties as those prescribed for the offense the commission of which was the object of the conspiracy."*

Title 18 U.S. Code, 1513 (e): *"Whoever knowingly, with the intent to retaliate, takes any action harmful to any person, including interference with the lawful employment or livelihood of any person, for providing to a law enforcement officer any truthful information relating to the commission or possible commission of any Federal offense, shall be fined under this title or imprisoned not more than 10 years, or both."*

Title 18 U.S. Code, 1513 (f): *"Whoever conspires to commit any offense under this section shall be subject to the same penalties as those prescribed for the offense the commission of which was the object of the conspiracy."*

Title 18 U.S. Code, 1514(b)(1): *"A United States district court, upon motion of the attorney for the Government, or its own motion, shall issue a protective order prohibiting harassment of a victim or witness in a Federal criminal case or investigation if the court, after a hearing, finds by a preponderance of the evidence that harassment of an identified victim or witness in a Federal criminal case or investigation exists or that such order is necessary to prevent and restrain an offense under section 1512 of this* title, other than an offense consisting of misleading conduct, or under section 1513 of this title."

(10) CIVIL RIGHTS

Title 18 U.S. Code, 249: HATE AND CRIMES, 242: DEPRIVATION OF RIGHT UNDER COLOR OF LAW, 245 (b) (B): FEDERAL PROTECTED ACTIVITIES

(11) VICTIM'S RIGHT:
Title 18 U.S. Code, 3771(a) (1), *"The right to be reasonably protected from the accused."*

(12) RELEASE OR DETENTION OF A DEFENDANT PENDING TRIAL:

Title 18 U.S. Code, 3142 *"The judicial officer may not impose a financial condition that results in the pretrial detention of the person."*

(13) MAJOR FRAUD AGAINST THE UNITED STATES

Title 18 U.S. Code, 1031

And the Title, 1343, gives district courts the jurisdiction to hear claims against the United States by Citizens of the United States for civil actions.

Also:
Amendment IX: "The enumeration in the Constitution, of certain right, shall not be construed to deny or disparage others retained by the people".

(And the usage of the pronoun of "ONE" and the determiner of "ANOTHER" in the 11th Amendment extends the court jurisdiction to hear the claim of "ALL" Citizens from their own State).

Amendment XI: "The judicial power of the United States shall not be construed to extend to any suit in law or equity, commenced or prosecuted against <u>ONE</u> of the United States by Citizens of <u>ANOTHER</u> State"

REASONS FOR GRANTING THE PETITION

"If you believe in your Bible, you must release your Prince from captivity, says your Lord."

And if you don't believe in Bible, you also must release the Prince from captivity, says your Constitution."

(From Hands on the Bible, a book by M.K.)

Respectfully submitted,

M. K.

Date

The Rule 30-4 of the Supreme Court states that in the most extraordinary circumstances a Justice is to review a motion of extension for a petition for a writ of certiorari. (Rule 30-4, Page 41). But the Court Clerk has returned my papers that were supposed to be reviewed by honorable Justice Ruth Ginsburg.

I believe that this motion includes in the most extraordinary circumstances because: (a) the courts have blocked me from filing on time and: (b) the courts have directly prolonged my thought process and harmed me financially and psychologically and they have diminished my abilities to file on a timing and proper manner.

My grievances against the Government officials, who support the Kidnapping that is allowed by their Bible and committed by their hero: George Washington, have been blocked many times.

I have claimed that some officials have committed Conspiracy to Defraud the United States and many other officials have committed Obstruction of justice by blocking the Conspiracy to be revealed because of their conflicts of interests in supporting the use of their own Bible and the figure of Washington in the Government.

OBSTRUCTION OF CRIMINAL INVESTIGATIONS:

Title 18 U.S. Code, 1510 (a): *"Whoever willfully endeavors by means of bribery to obstruct, delay, or prevent the communication of information relating to a violation of any criminal statute of the United States by any person to a criminal investigator shall be fined under this title, or imprisoned not more than five years, or both.*

OBSTRUCTION OF JUSTICE: Title 18 U.S. Code, 1505, 1506, 1512 (a) (B), 1512 (a) (2) (A), and 1519.

(If these documents are sent back again for the third time, by any person other than honorable Justice Ruth Ginsburg, to: *"Delay the investigation of crimes in progress and to prevent the communication of information that are revealed by Mr. K. relating to a violation of the criminal statute of the United States, to the Honorable Justice Ruth Ginsburg",* a complaint will be filed at the 8th Federal Court District against those who would have blocked this motion for Obstruction of Justice and Committing Conspiracy to block the investigation of major fraud against the United States).

WHEN RELIGION IS NOT SEPARATED FROM THE STATE OF MIND,

NO ONE WILL BE SAFE FROM THE STATES GOVERNED BY SUCH MINDS

Every hour 2 American lives are lost because of the Government and Corporations policies.

Churches, Corporations and individuals, which have funded or received funds and benefits from the Government are an accomplice in the crimes that have committed by their collaboration. Most of them have supported the Unconstitutional threats made toward the public and all of them have benefited financially from the policies that they have set, which have caused people to die by the minutes for the last 244 years!

The Kidnapping of the petitioner's child is the result of the support of racism by such organizations and entities. They have trained, encouraged or even recruited terrorists to attack and murder the people that are hated by their ideology.

(The Police who shoot people in the back, the terrorists who shot dead 49 people in gay club, shot 11 African American in church, shot 9 Jewish in synagogue recently, are terrorists who are recruited, schooled, and funded by Government chaplains, Church pastors and Corporations' executives who commit such crimes to protect their ideology and to secure their assets by their abusive economic policies).

THE TRIO CONSPRIACY TO COMMIT GENOCIDE

Churches, corporations and the government murder more than 30,000 Americans each year. They transfer the income of poor workers overseas, evict them in the streets from their homes, and purposely create a violent environment for them to be eliminated. The religious authorities have been committing the Genocide for 2019 years because it has been their religious duty to cause pain on poor people to gain wealth:

"Beat the Black in the Back" (To get rich, you are allowed to torture and abuse the poor because you are the superior race chosen by God). (Bible Luke: 12:47)

Churches encourage officials, employers and Capitalists to abuse poor people to get rich. And if poor workers and employees do not comply, they ought to be punished and eliminated. They have convinced people that the poor people, who are wondering in the streets, carry Satan and bad spirits and they deserve to be harmed and to be eliminated.

Just like the terrorist group of ISIS that believe they would be rewarded if they eliminated Satanic Americans, many Corporate Executives, who become Government officials, believe that they would be rewarded if they eliminate the Satanic Americans!

Blacks, Latinos, and Pagans are to serve the priests and judges and if they don't, they are to be punished severely. (Burnt alive, stoned to death, beaten with many blows, their living space restricted to the corner of the street or in prison, their food supply of Bison cut off, given poison gas, injected HIV, bombed from above or simply shot in the back).

By having their hands on their criminal ideology to take office, they are committed to commit the crime of Genocide.

They are committed to commit it.

LEGALLY STEALING THE NATION'S WEALTH

MAJOR FRAUD AGAINST THE UNITED STATES
[Title 18 U.S. Code, 1031, Title 18, 371, Title 18, 373(a) (c)]

Title 18, 373(c): "It is not a defense to a prosecution under this section that the person solicited could not be convicted of the crime because he lacked the state of mind required for its commission, because he was incompetent or irresponsible, or *because he is immune from prosecution or is not subject to prosecution".*

Many U.S. officials have committed Conspiracy to Defraud the United States by creating poverty, violence, crimes and terrorism, and by forcing thousands of Americans into homelessness and causing thousands to die from hunger, cold, violence, war and terrorism. They intentionally have increased the price of housing, shipped works overseas, gave free money to Private Bankers, diminished the value of workers' pay, and created the inflation and the high cost of living.

They have intentionally created the inflation to increase the value of their assets in housings and stock market and to increase the value of the assets of those who used such assets electing them in office, enabling them to own more houses, while such policies have lowered the value of the pay of millions of Americans and forcing them to lose their homes. To increase the value of their shares in companies, they have shipped millions of American jobs overseas to benefit from lower wages paid to foreign workers that have caused the loss of income for millions of Americans.

The officials have set policies that have transferred jobs to overseas and they have increased the cost of housing that have forced millions of Americans out of their jobs and homes and into homelessness of whom thousands die every year for not having income and home! While the wealthy officials have become wealthier to buy more of the houses that are lost by the thousands of Americans! To increase the income of a few, they made the majority of the United States Citizens to suffer and they purposely have increased the cost of living that has left so many lives behind.

They are aware that such economic policies cause the deaths of thousands every year (2 people die every hour!) but they knowingly continue such policies only to benefit themselves and to set favorable policies to benefit the wealthy groups who used their wealth electing them in office!

They have lowered the cost of productivity for a few at the loss of lives of so many!

The selfishness and ruthless character of the few in command, who set policies that only benefit their own tiny group of people in the cost of harming the lives of larger groups of people, is derived from their religious ideology that praises the tinny group of people over other larger groups of people who are called "pagan" people in their Bible. They are raised to praise the ideology that praises them; the tinny group of wealthy people, over many other groups of poor people. Their ideology commands them to be mean and savage toward many groups of people in order to gain their wealth! It even encourages them to kill their men and steal their women and children! (Bible, Deuteronomy 22:21, 20:13, 14 &Leviticus 25:44). Their

Bible does not abolish slavery and it gives them the right to enslave them, the poor "pagan" people, and that they could even hit their poor workers into submission! (Bible, Luke 12:47). And this is why officials don't care about the wellbeing of poor people because they are taught that poor people are "pagans" who are from "shithole" countries (As Mr. Trump calls them).

The Secretary of the Treasury, Mr. Steven Mnuchin, sets policies that increases the cost of housings and living and he transfers works and productivity overseas that causes hundreds of thousands of Americans to lose work, not being unable to afford the high cost of living and housing and forced into living in the streets, of which thousands perish every year!

He intentionally causes the inflation by allowing the Private Banks to loan billions of dollars from a source that doesn't even exist! With the help of Private Bankers, he prints billions of dollars that are injected into the economy every day to raise the prices and to increase the value of his assets and savings in Bank Stocks and housing, and to increase the value of the assets of his group friends of

Private Bankers and Real Stators whose assets helped appoint Mr. Mnuchin in office earning more than $200,000 a year and enabling him to set more favorable policies for them!

With the help of Mr. Mnuchin, Private Bankers increase their saving deposit 9 times over from a source that does not exist! Because officials, like Mr. Mnuchin, have allowed Private Bankers to set favorable rules for themselves in a private organization that is combined of their own Private Banks called Federal Reserve to fool the public thinking that it is a Governmental organization! They have made it a rule for themselves to loan 9 times more than their actual saving deposits! (If they have $1 billion in their saving, they are allowed to loan $10 billion more!). Allowing Private Bankers to set rules for themselves to loan money that they don't even have and allowing Private Bankers to make money out of NOTHING and exchange the paper money with the public's hard earned products is a Fraud against the people of the United States because the public sweat to earn to save while a few privates increase their own saving from NOTHING and they earn income out of NOTHING! The

Private Bankers are in charge of the public savings of billions of dollars that are earned from hard work and they use the public savings to add to their own savings 9 times over! They give themselves billions of dollars credit out of NOTHING to loan to people and to make billions without doing the actual work.

Selling papers as money from NOTHING automatically makes money for them by simply increasing their savings deposits 9 times out of NOTHING each time they loan. This in turn, raises the value of their shares in Private Banking in stock market. The more they loan, the more their saving deposits are raised from NOTHING and the more the value of their share will rise. Their savings are multiplied and more profit will be reported which will raise the value of their shares in stock market. Any time a Banker loans a $1, not only he benefits from the interests on the dollar that is loaned, he also profits from the 9 times raise of his saving deposits out of NOTHING! His savings will be increased 9 times OUT OF NOTHING and more money he is allowed to lend even if he doesn't have anything in his saving deposit! He also would raise the value of his stock shares because the interest earned from the dollar will be reported as income that increases his shares in stock market as well.

In addition, the interest that is earned from the loaned money create extra money in the market that are printed by Treasury for the Banks which increases the money supply and creates the inflation that raises all prices including the value of the Banks investments in many other sectors.

Private Bankers overflow their own savings deposit indefinitely out of NOTHING!

If their last saving deposit of let's say $10 million is loaned, not only they earn $1 million from interests on the loan, but also they give themselves an extra FREE $90 million dollars out of NOWHERE to loan! And once they loaned the $90 million, they would be given $900 million to loan! And the cycle continues indefinitely!

The free money that is added to the savings of Private Bankers to loan; the increase of Private Banks' savings 9 times over their actual savings out of NOTHING will cause:

1. Private Bankers to earn massive amount of money from interests on more money that will be loaned.

2. Private Bankers' savings of investments in housing, banking, and stock market will be increased infinitely and definitely. (The extra money made from interests on loans increase the money supply in the market that automatically increases Banks' investments and stock share values and their investments in real states and housings).

3. Private Bankers' payments to their employees are reduced instantly. (Banks savings and income are increased instantly, constantly, infinitely, and definitely but the amount of salaries they pay to their employees and workers are not increased instantly but is shrunk constantly because the value of dollar fades away when so much dollars are injected in the market by the free money that are given to Private Bankers from NOTHING, which is made into rules by their own private party called Federal Reserve).

4. Private Bankers' savings will be increased INFINITELY to INFINIT AMOUNT from NO AMOUNT!

In contrast, the free money that is added to the savings of Private Bankers cause:

1. People wages and salaries to shrink in value.
2. People's rents will be raised
3. People have to pay more for gas, car, home, clothes, food and medicine.
4. The value of housing and the cost of living would be increased, and people's pay would be decreased and people would be evicted from their home to live in the streets and:
5. People are forced to commit offences to make a living. (Once they are in the streets, they are forced to sell their body, sell drugs, or steal to survive or they are forced to commit suicide to ease their pain).
6. Causes inflation, poverty, violence, crimes, conflicts, wars and terrorism.
7. Causes millions to die from starvation, hunger and cold and it causes millions to be killed in violence, crimes, conflicts, wars and terrorism.

The Government, which is shaped by the Private Banks' and few wealthy campaign money, sides with a few wealthy groups with lots of savings allowing them to increase their own savings and income from ZERO amounts to INFIINITE amount while it ignores larger groups of people with lesser savings and it makes policies that decreases their income and savings to ZERO amount!

The Government helps increasing the savings of those with higher savings while it decreases the savings of millions with lower savings.

The saving of the poor people is decreased by the minute from the billions of dollars credits that are added to the saving deposits of the wealthy groups of people!

The official policies that transfers savings of the poor people to the savings of the wealthy Private groups, is Unconstitutional because:

1. The Government has given people with more savings the monopoly to created money for themselves out of NOTHING, and:

2. The Government has added billions to the savings of groups of people who have billions in savings, and:

3. The Government has caused the savings of hundreds of millions of other people to shrink as the result of billions given to the billionaires, and:

4. The Government has given money to people with lots of money and such a giving of money to rich people has caused poor people with lesser money to suffer dearly!

5. The Government has protected the rich making them richer by setting policies that have made poor people poorer.

6. The Government has given money to the wealthy people making them healthier while it has taken the health and the wealth from millions of people making them sick, poor and unhealthy! and:

7. The Government has given wealth to the wealthy making them healthier while it has taken the lives of thousands of poor people!

8. The Government intentions of: "harming poor people and stealing their savings and giving it to rich people" has been intentional because the

Government has proved by its ceremonial actions that their intention to harm the poor and benefit the rich has been ideological. (Because they respect Luke 12:47 that one race is superior and must abuse the poor race who is inferior).

9. The Government intentionally creates Poverty and it intentionally forces "Poor" "pagan" people into homelessness and forces people into committing crimes to make a living!

10. Then, the Government uses all of its force and energy, savings and G.D.P to protect and secure the wealth of the wealthy people from the poor people it has committed itself ideologically to abuse! And the Government abuses its victims even more by arresting them, imprisoning them and executing them to death by Trials or just letting them to be rotten in the corner of the streets!

Mr. Mnuchin seems to be intelligent enough to read his own official data of the "one thousand of people" who die every year from hunger and cold alone! Yet, he doesn't care how many lives of the "poor" people are wasted as long as the value of his assets and the assets of his group of friends, who gave him his job, are increased! He doesn't care about the loss of "poor" lives because he is raised to praise the Bible that praises him over so many other "poor" people and he is taught that he has the right to even steal their women and children!

From the confusing messages of his Bible of: "love your neighbor", "love your enemy", and "kill their men and take their women and children and belonging", Mr. Mnuchin seem to have picked the latter. And that's why he doesn't care about so many "poor" lives that are lost as the results of his decision making. In fact, he even is given credit and blessings by his religion for making such "poor" people to suffer because his religious book of Bible tells him that he owns them the "pagan" people and that he has to force them into submission!

Official's intentions to abuse poor people is intentional!

The increase of house prices is considered a good economic sign and that the economy is healthy, is growing, and it is good for the public! It is a good economic growth for sure but only for those who have investments in apartment buildings and housing. The economic measure, that measures the increase of house price as a good economic growth, only calculates the growth of the assets of the wealthy people as an economic measure. The majority of the United States citizens, who would be suffering from the higher rise of housing prices and rents or the high cost of living, are not included in the economists' calculations because their economic measure is based on how much treasure the Treasury will add to the savings of the Private Bankers!

Their economic measure is based on the increase of their own treasure!

The truth is that the advancement in technology must have lowered the cost of home building and it must have lowered the price of housing and making it much affordable for everyone and not making them unaffordable for everyone. (The price of homes must be lowered just like home appliances and cars). The reality is that the policy to keep increasing the housing prices is a threat for the safety of the public. It is Treason and a

Crime because it forces thousands of people into homelessness to literally be tortured to death! It makes it more difficult for majority of the Citizens of the United States to afford rent or housing, causing them to work ever more and it prevents thousands of them from being able to afford the high cost of living and housing that forces them into homelessness to suffer a miserable life, of whom thousands die, get killed or commit suicide to end their painful life.

The policies of transferring the production thousands miles away (And have the products being shipped back thousands of miles!), and the intentional creation of the inflation by giving free money to banks that increases the value of housing, food, gas, and medicine, only benefits a tinny group of people like Mr. Mnuchin, in the cost of harming millions of people dearly! The hundreds of thousands of people (The Homeless) who don't have any money to bribe any politician to care for them are left without any official voice in a system that money has become an incentive in setting rules and setting officials in the office!

"Poor" people, who have no homes, assets, or income, are treated differently from rich people, who have more wealth; home, assets, income, and saving deposits to loan, by the wealthy Government officials who have used the wealth of the wealthy people to be elected in office!

Not only the poor action of rich officials, such as Mr. Mnuchin, is Unconstitutional for treating "poor" people differently from rich people, but it also is a Conspiracy against the "poor" people because officials such as Mr. Mnuchin or Mr. Trump officially have made commitment to commit crimes against the "poor" people by taking Oath to so many threats that are made against such "pagan" poor people in their Bible! They believe that "poor" people are "pagan" nationals from "Shithole" counties who ought to be treated as subjects! (Mr. Trump calls the poor people "shithole" because his Bible calls them "pagan" and "worthless").

Government officials have given billions of dollars to the people (The Bankers) with billion dollars TO BE SAVED in their savings from NOTHING, while people with NO SAVINGS are given NOTHING TO BE SAVED! (With the exception of food stamps and very limited housings and healthcare).

Billions of dollars are added to the SAVINGS of the billionaires from NOTHING while people with NO SAVINGS are given NOTHING TO BE SAVED!

People with more savings are given the authority to create savings and income for themselves out of NOTHING, and they are given the authority to print money for themselves out of NOWHERE, which has lowered the value of the pay of poor people and has emptied them from their savings for paying too much for the high costs of living. People with more savings are given the authority to send the works of poor people overseas and they intentionally have raised the cost of living and housing that has emptied thousands of poor people from their income and savings that has forced them into homelessness.

Homeless people with no savings:

1.   Are not able to set policy for themselves.

2. Are not able to pay to bribe any politician into office to set favorable policy for them.

3. Are not able to create job or income for themselves.

4. Are not able to adjust their salaries or incomes.

5. Are not able to create saving for themselves out of NOTHING

6. Are not able to reduce the cost of living and housings or rent

7. Homeless are to suffer and die by the policies that are made by the help of the savings of the people with billions in savings who:

1. Are allowed to create savings for themselves out of NOTHING

2. Are allowed to set polices for themselves and for the poor people

3. Are allowed to adjust salaries for poor people, employees and workers

4. Are allowed to transfer the jobs of poor people overseas

5. Are allowed to increase the price of their houses for poor people

6. Are allowed to evict poor people from their homes into the streets

7. Are allowed to bribe politicians into office to make favorable policies for them

8. Are allowed to take poor people savings by intentionally creating the inflation

9. Are allowed to make policies that transfers the savings of poor people to rich people

10. Are allowed to set policies to create poverty, violence, crimes and terrorism that tortures and kills mostly poor people.

11. Are allowed to make threats to poor people officially

Using the ideology of religious groups, by swearing an Oath to their religious book, in order to promote and benefit from the belief (Collecting money and votes in Churches for example) and to benefit from the wealth of the religious groups (A) and:

Using the savings of the wealthy groups (Private Bankers) in order to be positioned in office to increase their savings (B) and:

Setting policies to create more savings for own and for the wealthy groups knowing that such policies empties the savings of poor groups and tortures and kills many groups of people with no saving at all(C), is the Conspiracy and the Major Fraud the officials, such as Mr. Mnuchin and Mr. Trump have committed against the United States.

The officials:

1. Have legislated favorable rules, or administered or executed laws favorably with respect to religious persons (John, Paul and George), and:
2. They have legislated, administered or executed laws to benefit the rich while harming the lives of so many poor Americans, and:
3. They have respected a particular religion (Bible's), religious persons and a figure who has committed child abuse, kidnapping and terrorism (George Washington), and:
4. They have made threats toward poor people in their Oath, and:
5. They have abused people verbally calling them "pagan" and "shithole", and"

6. They have created poverty, violence and crimes and terrorism that have caused the torture and murder of millions of Americans as well as millions of other "pagan" nationals inside and outside the country.

The officials economical polices and their verbal and ceremonial abuse and threats that has harmed millions of the citizens of the United States is a Conspiracy and Major Fraud against the United States and such officials must be prosecuted for their INTENTIONAL INTENTIONS of harming the citizens of the United States!

Not only they have acted Unconstitutional for siding with religious persons and treating rich and poor unequally, but also they have committed Treason because they have knowingly caused millions without wealth or religion to suffer and die by setting policies that have emptied them form their work, home and savings! (Poor people who became homeless and died, women who became homeless and were forced into prostitution, homosexuals who are not religious and were hated and killed, or the "pagan" nationals of African Americans, Native Americans,

Latinos who lost work, income, housing and were evicted from their home to became homeless and were forced to commit offences to make a living and were killed or suffered in prisons for selling drugs, selling their body or for stealing to survive.

The accused officials can't argue that they didn't know about the outcome of their policies that have harmed so many poor people because they have committed to harm the poor "pagan" people in office! They have called them names and they have respected others who have called them names as well! (George Washington and General Lee abused African Americans physically and verbally and they are praised by Mr. Trump and his party members).

They have made threats toward poor people because they are sworn into the threats that are made toward such people in their Bible. Their policies that have harmed poor people have been intentional because it has been ideological!

By their intentional oral and physical ceremonial action, they have shown that they had the intention to harm certain groups of Americans who are hated by their belief.

They have used the religious ideology to collect wealth and they have used wealth to collect votes to shape the political system in a way that people like themselves, with more assets who believe in the same religious ideology, have a much stronger chance in being elected in office and therefore to have a much stronger voice in the Government than people without assets who don't have a religious ideology. (Money collected from Churches used for selecting officials who have given Churches federal funds or the donations that are given to their religious political party from wealthy or religious people or religious organizations).

Mr. Mnuchin and Mr. Trump's policies have always been based on benefiting own and benefiting the certain groups who helped them being selected in office. They are serving themselves and not the country as they claim. They are not risking their lives like soldiers to serve their country.

They are taking the lives of the citizens of their country by their service!

They are not risking their lives for the people, they are taking the lives of the people!

Such Bankers and Real Stators value their own gross income over the safety of many others because they believe in their own gross threats that are made in their ideological book against so many "pagan" and "shithole" people! Their belief values the security of their savings above the safety of so many others! (Bible says that people like Trump and Mnuchin are the descendant of the free women and that they have the right to abuse and enslave many others who are the descendant of the bound women!).

STEALING WEALTH FROM NATIONS LEGALLY

Officials, such as Mr. Mnuchin and Mr. Trump, have been making policies that have forced many other people of many other nations into poverty as well! Just like the poverty that they have caused for the 44 million citizens of our beloved country, many other countries have also been affected by their policies and they have become so poor that thousands of their citizens are forced to migrate or they are forced to be recruited into terrorist organizations to make a living! Just like our dear fellow poor-ed citizens, who are recruited into Arm forces to kill to make a living, many other countries' poor people are also recruited in terrorist Arm forces to kill many poor Americans who are recruited in Arm forces killing them.

The corrupt policies that are made by corrupt officials, corrupts the system internally and it corrupt the systems internationally forcing millions to live in poverty that provoke violence, crime and terrorism that harms mostly the poor population of the world and the poor citizens of the United States. People all over the world are forced to commit offences to make a living once they are forced into poverty because they are left with no other options. Here is how the corrupt Government officials and Private Bankers have created poverty, violence, crimes and terrorism in the world:

STEALING LAND RESOURCE

For centuries the Western Private Bankers have been stealing the resource of nations by using swords and guns in their violent conquests. In parallel with their violent way of war to accumulate the wealth of nations, they also have been using their gentle way of loaning their currency to nations to accumulate their wealth!

They printed paper as money and loaned it to many nations or even offered them their paper money as a gift to internationalize their currency. Once their currency was internationalized and nations used their currency as an international exchange to trade goods with other nations, the Private Banks mass produced their currency, printed cheaply out of paper, and they exchanged their currency with the riches of the world! (Papers of Dollars or Pounds were given to collect Gold and Silver of the World!). They mass produced their currency and exchanged their papers with the riches of the world!

They printed papers as money and went into the world shopping!

No sword, gun, shackles, chains or force is needed to steal the wealth and human from nations. They simply print money out of paper and gently exchange the papers as money with the wealth of nations!

Poor countries can't just print Dollars or Euro to go shopping in the world. They have to sweat to produce a product in order to exchange with the Western countries while the Western Private Bankers don't need to work to gain the products or resources of the poor nations. They simply print money out of paper and exchange the papers with nations' hard earned products or their resources! This is the main reason that the rich people are getting richer and poor people ever getting poorer.

The U.S. officials have been printing billions of dollars out of papers for the Private Bankers and they have gone into the world shopping! They have injected trillions of dollars into the world economy and trillions dollars' worth of resources; TONS of materials, have been imported into the U.S. from other 194 nations and were added to the assets of Private Bankers and Real Stators (Such as Mr. Mnuchin and Mr. Trump) while most of the other 194 counties only gained trillions OUNCES/GRAMS of paper!

The food on the table of the hungry poor nations is transferred to feed the fat bellies of the rich American Bankers! (Who simply print money out of paper from a source they don't even have!).

The injection of the paper money into the world economy causes the inflation that decreases the value of workers' pay while it raises the cost of living, housing and stock market shares that primarily benefits Western Private Bankers, Real Stators, and Weapon Manufacturers who own shares in such companies and profit from the loans and the sales to people all over the world by the international branches of Private Banks and other companies in many countries. (Investors in weaponry sell more weapons to countries which are gone to war over the lift over of what is left from their limit-ed resources while investors in Real State and Banking profit from the more sales of houses and businesses and loans that are given to the wealthy immigrants who flee their conflicted country to work in the West).

Poor nations exchanging their desperately needed food with the Private Bankers paper money makes them ever poorer because they simply exchange their TONS OF FOOD with KILLO GRAMS OF PAPERS! (Even by weight they lose in the exchange!). Their bananas, coffee or lobsters are exchanged with papers of Dollars, Pounds, Euros or Yens). Poor nations lose in the exchange because they don't control the exchange. The Western Private Bankers do! The corrupt finance offices have set favorable rules for Private Banks to print as much as they wish! Banks are allowed to loan 9 times more than their total saving assets! The Private Banks, that control the Public exchange and have branches all over the world, have made it a rule for themselves to create money and savings out of NOTHING and they turn the NOTHING into billions of Dollars every day and they print trillions of Dollars every year!

The NOTHING will become trillions of the papers valued as money that are imported into poor countries and trillions worth of their mineral and products are exported into the Western rich countries!

The NOTHING:

1. Creates trillions of dollars for Private Bankers out of NOTHING inside the country, and :
2. The NOTHING, creates trillions of dollars for the Private Bankers outside the country that:
   a. Increases own assets and savings while reduces the pay paid to workers and:
   b. Transfers trillion tons of food, product, mineral and resource from poor nations to the wealthy nations for FREE!

Not only the Private Bankers transfer the wealth of the poor people to the saving accounts of the wealthy people inside the U.S. (By printing too much Dollars out of no resource and loaning it as money that devalue the pay of employees and workers and by increasing the cost of living and housing), but also the Private Banks transfer the wealth from poor nations to the saving accounts of the wealthy nations!

The Government official, such as Mr. Mnuchin, a Banker who is appointed in Governmental with the help of the assets of Private Bankers, says to the Private Bankers: "Don't worry. We let you loan as much as you wish even if you don't have the money to loan. We screw people together to steal their resources with the paper money. As long as you print lots of money in the market causing the increase of the value of my shares in stocks, Banking and Housing, and as long as you guys help me be selected in office making donations for my campaign, I am on your side and you are allowed to loan money even if you don't even have the money to loan!".

It really hurts knowing that most of the WEALTH that is used to corrupt officials to transfer the wealth of poor people to the wealthy people, were accumulated corruptly in the first place!

Most of the savings and the wealth of the Private Bankers of today were accumulated illegally through stealing and abusing poor people by their ancestors' violent conquests.

They conquered lands and they stole humans and resources of their lands and they force labored the stolen humans on the stolen lands to accumulate the wealth that were passed on to their next generation, which are held by the Private Bankers of today. Through heritage, most of the wealth of the wealthy that mostly were generated by abuse, transferred to the wealth of the Private Bankers of today. (Which causes more abuse! The wealth that is primarily accumulated by abuse is used to abuse even more today through private banking!).

And much of other part of the wealth was accumulated smoothly through Private Banking that turned paper into money and exchanged the paper money with the tangible treasure of the world!

They gave them paper and took their Pearl, Gold, Diamond and Silver!
Or they inserted bullets into them to extract what was theirs!

(Much of the southern states of California, Louisiana, Nevada, New Mexico, and Arizona and Alaska seem to have been stolen the same way!).

Stealing from people by exchanging paper with their resources shouldn't be a surprise at all because the Westerners have a habit of taking things and giving nothing in exchange. (American Indians were given nothing when thousands of them were slaughtered by the Westerners who took their Golds when they first arrived on their continent and millions of Africans were given only chain and shackles when they were stolen from their continent to work on the stolen Indian land).

Through wars, conquest or by Private Banking, using hard wares or soft wares, forcibly taking or kindly giving, (The free loaning of paper money as gift), the wealth of decent, poor, hardworking people have been transferred to the wealth of the greedy aggressors who made the poor poorer and the wealthy wealthier enabling many wealthy to use their illegally saved wealth in bribing officials (That is called donation) or to invest their illegally accumulated wealth in Private Banking enabling themselves to loan trillion dollars made out of NOTHING to continue their gentle stealing!

The corruptly generated wealth, savings and assets of Private Bankers are held mostly by religious white males, who are Congressmen, Presidents, Judges, Justices, Executives, Kings, Priests or Pope.

Women, gays, or "pagan" nationals around Israel such as Africans, Palestinians or Yemenis hold a tiny portion of the savings, wealth and authority in Governments or religion organizations because the Governments, that mostly are made of religious wealthy and male officials, have promoted and valued their own religion, gender, race, and nationality above many other, genders, races, nations, religions and none believers.

And because the religious, wealthy, male officials have promoted the ideology that commanded them to gain the wealth of certain people by hurting and abusing them, the savings and the wealth of the white male western assets is accumulated in a much greater quantity than of the certain groups of people who are hated and threatened by the ideology.

And, the number of white male westerns in authority of Private Banking, Government, Business and Religion became much greater than the numbers of races, genders or nationals who were hated and harmed by their ideology.

The corrupt Governments' officials used religious ideology to suppress many groups of people and nations for more than 2019 years and that is why the wealth and status is not distributed equally among people or nations (Bible for example values Israel above other nations or it values men over women. Bible: "women are not to hold authority over man but to be quiet. Slaves are to serve their masters. Men of nations from around Israel are to be killed and their women, children, land and belonging are to be stolen").

The respect of Governments' officials for Bible, Quran and Torah has been the main cause of inequality, poverty, violence, racism, crimes, wars and terrorism that have

tortured and killed millions of Americans and people
around the world.

Allowing the wealthy men with the most savings to create wealth and savings from PAPER or NOTHING at all, and allowing Private Bankers to exchange their papers to conquer the treasure of the world creating poverty, violence, terrorism, war and crimes that have tortured and murdered thousands of Americans is the Conspiracy and the Major Fraud against the United States committed by officials, like Mr. Mnuchin who have committed to the Bible to commit crimes against the citizens of the United States by skillfully entering into the Treasury and smoothly have access to the treasures of the world.

STEALING HUMAN RESOURCE

Western politicians, of whom mostly are male Bankers, such as French President Mr. Macron or the U.S. Treasure secretary Mr. Mnuchin, can't use chain and shackles to steal Africans from their "pagan" nations any more as they did 150 years ago. Nor they could conquer any "poor" nation by force in wars in order to steal their resource, wealth or their men. So they devised the smooth way of loaning nations their soft paper currency to steal their wealth. And they kindly send invitations to them inviting their intellectuals and wealthy people to enjoy the Western lifestyle by working and living in the West.

Every year, thousands of wealthy people or intellectuals like engineers, doctors, nurses, or skilled workers, from poor nations are offered to work in the United States. They transfer with them years of their nations' resources that were invested in their education and training or their savings that will be added to the wealth of the U.S. wealthy groups when they purchase or invest in the west. The stealing of poor nations' intellectuals and wealthy people is another gentle form of stealing the wealth and resource from nations which the Western economists call "human investment!

Just like the stealing of the savings and the income of the poor people of the U.S. by the officials such as Mr. Mnuchin, that creates poverty in the country, the stealing of the intellectuals and wealthy people from poor nations around the world creates poverty in their county. Nations, which are faced with the poverty caused by the replacement of their food with paper money, lose more of their land resource and they lose more of their men power when their wealthy and educated people take their wealth and their education with them out of their country. Their poor people are left behind to deal with the shortage of investment, wealth and education that transfers to the west through migration.

Mr. Mnuchin is very well aware that an increase in poverty means an automatic increase in violence and crimes in such nations and he knows very well that millions of poor people suffer from hunger and die from the poverty and the violence that is caused by his gentle offerings of money loans or Green cards. And he knows that such gentle policies endanger the U.S. safety and security causing thousands of Americans to die while only it secures the wealth of the wealthy people such as himself! (It only helps % 0.001 of the population).

Knowing the history of exploitation of poor countries by the west through violent conquests, and learning of the westerners' tricks of gentle offerings of loans, jobs and Green cards that are designed to empty nations from land and human resources, forces such nations to be hostile toward the western policies that endangers their lives. Just like the poor people in the U.S., who are forced into poverty and are forced to commit offences to make a living, many nations are forced into poverty and they are forced to commit offences to make a living. Nations that are forced into poverty for centuries by the west, are forced to commit offences against the west to survive! Just like the poor people inside the country, who are left to be rotten in the corner of the streets and who are forced into selling drugs or selling their bodies to make a living, many nations make money out of selling drugs, prostitution, Kidnapping, and terrorism to survive. And many leaders of such nations, who are raised in a society without education and wealth, join gangs and terrorist organizations and eventually become leaders who turn their country an enemy of the west. (Such as Taliban of Afghanistan, Clergies of Iran, Gadhafi of Libya, or the leaders of North Korea).

Just like the poor people of the United States, who are drawn into poverty and are left with no other choice but to commit offense to survive, many poor nations that are drawn into poverty would also be left with no other choice but to commit offences to survive. (In the U.S. many poor people are forced into arm forces to make a living and many more join gangs, steal or commit crimes to make a living as well). They would take extreme measures of earing income and fighting back by being recruited in terrorist organizations attacking Americans and the Westerners. They are forced to build up their Arm forces to secure their resources and borders and fight back with the Western hostile policies that have been set by the corrupt U.S. and Western politicians who don't mind hostility, conflicts and wars because it is good for their business! They would benefit from conflicts because they loan more money, sell more weapons and products, and they take advantage of nations' wealthy and intellectuals who are willing to flee their unstable nations to live in the West. And of course such an Arm build up by poor nations make it easier for the corrupt U.S. politicians to sell to the public their defense budget increase, which of course increases their income by selling more weaponry and loans, which cost the poor tax payers) The stealing of the wealth of poor people inside the country and the stealing the wealth of other nations and transferring the wealth to the saving accounts of the wealthy western people causes:

1. Poor nations to be recruited in international terrorist organizations killing innocent people and Americans and:
2. Poor nations to produce drugs that causes suffering and death in the U.S. and the west (Like Afghanistan producing opium and Colombia producing cocaine) and:
3. Causing arm races among people inside the country and among nations spending more of their savings or G.D.P on weaponry and gun, security and defense that:

4. Causes poverty, crime, violence and terrorism abroad and inside the county such as Oklahoma bombing or school shootings that directly are derived from:

a. Setting policies that transfers the wealth from majority of people to a few rich people and:

b. Spending peoples' savings and G. D.P. on weaponry, arm forces and security rather than creating jobs, education, healthcare, housing, nutrition or family values.

The stealing from poor people by the wealthy people inside the county, and the stealing from the poor nations by the wealthy nations in the world creates hostile environment among the individual citizens internally and internationally. People savings are wasted on walls, doors, locks, barb wires, security cameras, alarms, police, security, guns and bullets, and armies. People are over worked to catch up with the high cost of living causing many to live with loneliness and depression. People are expelled from family and communities, raised by single patents and use more of alcohol and drugs and become mentally and bodily sick. Poverty brings illnesses, sickness hunger and desperation, loneliness, depression and pain that forces people to commit offences to make a living or to rid of their pain. Some commit suicide, to end their pain, and some join gang groups, terrorist organizations to fight the Injustice that were inflicted on their life or they compete with the corrupted wealthy groups in stealing others' wealth! People are forced to commit offences to escape from their pain by attacking and shooting others in schools, malls, church, synagogue, or casinos. Violent groups of mafias, gangs or corrupted religious organizations and political groups are shaped inside the country or violent groups of western allies of NATO, Russian-Chinese, Al Qa eda-Isis groups are shaped among nations spending more of their poor peoples' resources and G.D.P on arms and arm forces to either compete in having more access to the resources and the G.D.P of other nations or to secure their owns'. Gangs, Police and individual citizens spend their savings on gun and bullets and security and nations spend their resources and G.D.P. on weaponry, guns, bullets and bombs, warships, submarines, air, nuclear and other war crafts that increase tensions, conflicts and war and terrorism inside counties and among nations.

The exploitation of nations by Private Bankers (Who are %0.001 of the population of the world) causes nations to spend billions of their G.D.P. on Military and Weaponry which draws their nations into poverty which creates violence, crimes and terrorism that harms Americans as well. (Russians and NATO competition to have access to the resources of many nations between them is another example of nations wasting their G.D.P. to feed their nuclear arm ambition rather than feeding their poor populations). Thousands of Americans lose their life either by wars, terrorist attacks, in shootings, over dose of drugs, in gang and violence, or in accidents caused by extra traffics that is created by unnecessary shipments of works abroad, or simply for being hungry and cold and for not having home and savings. (The Government seems to have prioritized the spending on Weaponry build up to profit the gun and weapon manufacturers rather than feeding and homing their homeless population).

The flow of the wealth, the wealthy and intellectuals to the West increases the Real State value of the wealthy officials such as Mr. Trump, who benefit from the more demands caused by the immigrants in the market. There would be more customers coming into courtly who profit the official Bankers, such as Mr. Mnuchin, who benefits by loaning more mortgages. Mr. Trump is also aware of the value of immigrants' intellect, wealth, skill and labor and that is why he works closely with Mr. Mnuchin in the stealing of the intellectuals and the wealthy people from the poor countries Mr. Trump calls "shithole" countries!

CREATING VIOLENCE

To sell more houses, to loan more money, and to sell more guns, they destabilize nations' economy and politics so their wealthy and educated people are willing to migrate to the West to invest or work for them in the west. (They even profit from the low wages paid to the poor immigrant workers which brings down the pay of native workers as well. And millions of dollars are saved from not providing regulated services such as insurance or paid over time and vacation to undocumented immigrants). They use force, manipulation, bribery, and they provide weapons, intelligence and money to dictators, criminals and terrorists in order to increase the demand for their product and services mainly loans, which cheaply is made out of toilet paper into dollars, and weapons. Supporting Saddam Hossain of Iraq, Saudi and Iranian King or Osama ben Laden and Taliban are few examples. The savings and G.D.P. of the U.S. citizens are spent on supporting Saudi Arabia's war in Yemen, dismembering journalists, and suppressing thousands of people who are suppressed and tortured in Saudi prisons. The same way the U.S. supported Iranian, Iraqis and other dictators for centuries. The support of the violent acts of Israel is also another example of wasting U.S. G.D.P. and savings and endangering the people of the U.S. only to benefit the Private Bankers, Real stators and weapon manufacturers, of whom mostly are Bible believers. Conflicts between nations Russia -Ukraine, Israel-Palestine, Iran-Saudi Arabia, and the conflicts among gangs-gangs and People-Police inside the country is good for business because more guns and weapons, loans, equipment and machinery which are sold to secure people and nations or to replace damaged infrastructures.

People of nations are attacked by their arm forces and they are hit with bullets and bombs in wars or people are attacked inside the country by their Police force with fists and bullets. They promote violence and hatred through:

a. Preaching and promoting violent versus of their Bible and:

b. Promoting violent figures who committed violent crimes and:

c. Promoting violent policy of Policing the nation and:

d. Promoting violent policy of Policing nations and:

e. Promoting violent policy of selling violent tools to the nation and nations and:

f. Promoting violence and conflicts among the nation and promoting conflicts among nations. (Promotion of religious racism inside the country and creating religious conflicts among nations).

Too safe never is good for business.

People of nations ought to be insecure, conflicted, desperate, and depended on the wealth held by the tinny people in command so:

1. They could be exploited to work for lower wages and:

2. They are forced to migrate and:

3. They are forced to sell their goods for cheap and:

4. They are forced to exchange their goods with Private Bankers papers and:

5. They are forced to spend their savings on guns and security and:

6. They are forced to be depended on the loans of Private Bankers to buy home, car, business and economic developments and most of all:

7. PEOPLE NEVER BE AT PEACE TO UNDERSTAND THE LIES, THE FRAUD AND THE CONDPIRACY OF THE CORRUPT POLITICIANS AND:

8. THEY ARE MADE BUSSY WORKING THAT NEVER GROUP TO TAKE ACTIONS AGAINST THEIR CORRUPTION.

Private Bankers open branches all over the world and juice nation's savings and make them to be dependent on them for survival. People and nations are made poor, unstable and weak to be depended to the wealth and savings of the Private Banks to survive. (People inside the country and nations are made to be dependent on the loans of Private Banks to start a business, purchase car, house, to study, and to buy equipment and machinery). It is much easier to steal from weak and uneducated people and nations by paying them less and buying their product cheap or just buying their product with their paper money that they produce by own Private Banks! People and nations will have no choice but to work for minimum wage and pay the high cost of living or they know they end up in the street to be rotten or nations will know that they face sanctions, starvations and wars if they don't comply with the Private Bankers gentle loan, Green cards and job offerings.

Government officials are used to the stealing from "pagan" nations' resource and man power because they are raised to praise the stealing from birth and their generation has been praising such policy for at least 2019 years. Their economic policy is based on their ideological belief of beating, killing and destructing of "pagan" nations to gain their wealth and they have been beating, murdering, dismembering, Kidnapping and destroying nations to steal their wealth for more than 2019 years.

They made nations unstable, weak and unsecure so they are in need of purchase of gun for security and defense and they are made to be depended on Western loans, guns and products for survival.

Controlling the exchange by printing billions of dollars in paper money every day and exchanging the papers with the products of poor countries weakening their economy and forcing their wealthy people and their intellectuals to flee to the west to invest or work becoming good customers for Real Stators and Bankers has become a norm for politicians like Mr. Trump and Mr. Mnuchin, who would pay much lesser for training and education of their immigrant employees because they have other countries paid for their education already!

Mr. Trump and Mr. Mnuchin:

1. Ship works overseas
2. Increase the price of houses
3. Print paper out of NOTHING and steal nations resources and wealth by their counterfeiting of turning paper into money and:

4. They steal nations' intellectuals and wealthy people to increase the assets of their own housings and stock shares in banking, while ignoring the fact that such intellectuals are desperately needed by their country to help raise their own G.D.P or education, which are necessary for balancing the growth of their population and reducing their poverty that their country suffering from dearly. And:

5. They intentionally create conflict among people and among nations and they intentionally created poverty, violence, crimes and terrorism to profit from the chaos they created in communities and among nations to sell more guns, weapons, loans, and to increase their assets in stock market and real states, to create inflation, and to attract foreign wealth, immigrants, and intellectuals.

Harming the lives of others only to increase own savings is intentional because it is ideological! Mr. Trump and Mr. Mnuchin are sworn into office by Bible that calls the poor nations "pagan nations" and Mr. Trump specifically calls the poor countries "shithole" counties because their belief commands them to disrespect and harm such nationals and steal their women, children and their animals! (Bible, Deuteronomy 22:21, 20:13, 14 &Leviticus 25:44).

The stealing of resource and human of "pagan" nations have been the ideology of officials like Mr. Trump or Mr. Mnuchin, who praised such ideology in office. They also have praised figures who committed the crimes that is provoked by their ideology.

They have been praising "the criminals" who had followed the books' criminal ideology and had committed the crimes of the Kidnapping and child abuse that was required to be committed by the believers! George Washington or General Lee and many other figures, who have committed felonies, are praised by the Government. A man, who had contained the Independence of 100s of humans and traded and abused children, is praised as a hero of Independence! Not only the officials make commitments to commit crimes in their ritual ceremonies, but also they praise figure or group of friends who have committed major offences! (Mr. Trump praising Mr. Madaford, who committed crimes and him being reluctant to accept a murder committed by the Saudi dictator are samples of Mr. Trump's praise of the wealth and status of the wealthy criminals who have committed major offences).

The officials have committed Conspiracy and Major Fraud against the United States by:

1. *Making commitments to the criminal commands and:*

2. *For praising the criminal commanders and:*

3. *For sending people job overseas to benefit from lower payments to workers and add what is saved to the executive incomes, who donate to their campaign:*

4. *For increasing the price of houses to benefit from the high rise in prices and:*

5. *For printing money out of NOTHING to transfer the saving of people and nations and adding it to their own savings and:*

6. *For stealing nations' intellectuals and wealthy people to increase their own assets and savings and:*

7. *For intentionally creating conflict among people and among nations and for intentionally creating the poverty, violence, crimes and terrorism to profit from the chaos they created in communities and among nations to sell more weapons, loans, increase their assets in stock market and real states, and to steal foreign wealth, immigrants, and intellectuals and:*

8. *All above construed the Conspiracies that harmed thousands of Americans who died from homelessness, thousands who were killed in wars, conflicts, and terrorism, and thousands who died or killed from drug use, violence and crimes, and thousands who died in traffic accidents that were created by the extra traffics that created by the policy of shipping productions thousand miles away).*

They don't follow mother Teresa's path who gave to "poor" countries. They follow the Washington's path who took from the "pagan" "shithole" nations! Their goal of gaining others' wealth in the cost of the loss of so many lives has been their religious ideology for years. By the promotion of the Bible in office and by having respect for General Lee or Washington, people are made to be ignorant toward the violent commands of the Bible and they are made to ignore the violent crime committed by Washington and Lee. They are raised to praise one group of people over many other groups and they are raised to praise one nation above many other nations. They are raised to value one religion above other religions from birth and they are raised from young age (From Boy scouts) to be patriotic, nationalists, and follow the criminal ideology of the Bible so that the Bible-ists in command could take advantage of people's belief and interests to conflict them with other people and nations and send them to wars to accumulate the wealth of nations in the cost of wasting millions of their lives!

The U.S. stealing of wealth and man power from Guatemala and Honduras makes them poor and unsafe causing them to migrate to the U.S. just to be separated from their children at the border and being thrown in prison while they are humiliated as violent immigrants who steal jobs from Americans!

.

CREATING A LIFESTYLE THAT IS BASED ON WASTE

Destroying local small businesses and living communities to force people to travel longer distances from home to work in order to sell more gas, cars, tires, and siding with giant corporations destroying historical local communities and turn them into giant apartment buildings or sky scrapers to force people to pay for rent rather than live in their parents' house is another Major Fraud against people. (People used to live as a family in one building working downstairs in the family business and live upstairs. Now they are made to drive far to work and pay rent. People's savings are wasted on transportation, the time of travel, and high rent).

Creating the lifestyle that wastes more to consume more also creates more accidents and deaths, more depression, loneliness, homelessness, crime and violence, more usage of guns, drugs and alcohol, prostitution, and of course the more of shootings at schools and malls and casinos, and more of the shootings of people in the backs! (Shooting blacks in the backs by police).

To benefit more from the more sale of guns and weapons, vehicle and equipment and materials and products, not only the society is made to be in conflict with itself so there will be more need for security, police, arm forces, warships, tanks, artilleries, aircrafts, guns, bullets, barb wires, doors, locks, keys, alarms, cameras, chains, (And billion dollars border walls!), but also the society needs to waste more to consume more of the Private Bankers', Real Stators', and Manufacturers' loans, apartment buildings, and products respectively.

Besides, there is a double profit in such policy: A society that is not at rest does not have time to learn who is screwing them. People are occupied with conflicts, over worked, their interests is directed toward too much of entertainments, drugs and alcohol so:

1. More guns, security equipment's, car parts, Tabaco, drug, alcohol, video games, movies, sports gear, protein and materials are sold and:

2. People are amused, occupied and entertained so they are distracted and could not be informed easily about the conspiracy and fraudulent activities of the corrupted officials.

3. People amused or conflicted to be separated so they could not easily unite to form an opposing force to protest, strike or create a decent political force that would eliminate their corruption. (The low incomes in France protest in groups but in the U.S. over a million homeless retreat into bushes to die alone. France's politic is more liberal but the conservative U.S. politics follows Bible's commands in forcing workers into submission or leaving them to be rotten in the bushes).

People are kept in poverty, weak and dependent on Private Banker's savings and loans. They are over worked, they are made to pay too many payments, made to drive long distances, kept amused with too many entertainments; porn, drug and alcohol, and they are made weak, sick and poor to be conflicted among themselves making it much harder for them to learn and understand the conspiracy and the fraud of those who are emptying their pockets and makes it more complicated to unite as a strong force to fight corruption and Injustice. (That is why the corruption lasted 244 years! Even Pakistan had a women Prime minister but the U.S. lacks behinds in female leader ship and still prints its currency with picture of men because Bible commands that women cannot take authority over men. The politicians' and Judge's Bible says: "Workers must be quiet and work only. And women must shut up and can't tell men what to do and they should respect their husbands as God!"-Ephesians 5:22). Insecurity in society is a necessity for the success of Private Bankers, Real Stators and Gun manufacturers.

Too safe wouldn't be too safe for business.

The safety and security of the lives of a great majority is sacrificed to secure the savings of the tinny people!

Creating a culture of depression and loneliness along with hardship of work and living by the high cost of living and traveling far distances, replacing education with entertainments, drugs and alcohol, causes families to be worn out, conflicted, separated, divorced, children raised to be abused in poverty and raised by single parents who would end up shooting at schools to kill for excitement or ease their pain. People reject abusive religions and leaders and they live a lonely harsh life that cause depression and desperation that causes people taking desperate measures hurting own and others in suicides, homicides or shootings and terrorist attacks to be relieved from their depression or desperation and pain.

Mr. Trump and Mr. Mnuchin created all the above policies that created homeless, prostitute, drug addicts, criminals and gangs, drug dealers and sex traffickers, pimps and sex slaves, rapes, theft, robberies ‹over a million prison inmates, too many police, security, camera, lock, door, chain, barbed wire, fence, wall, security, bullet proof jackets. They use people's resources (Taxes) to create the problems and insecurity and then they spend more of people's resources (Taxes and people own income spent for security) to solve the problem by security! Their policies created so much waste and friction and the loss of G.D.P. and savings and they wasted so many lives and they have caused so much suffering only to benefit own.

INEFFICIENT TRANSPORTAION

To benefit from the sale of more tires, gas, motor oil, cars, trucks, copper, steal and so on, and in order to sell more crude oil, tart, asphalt, cement, road machineries and construction materials or equipment, they have betrayed the public by promoting cars and roads as a good choice of transportation over more efficient transportation of electric trains and rail roads. And combined with the increase of the extra traffics, that is caused by the shipments of productions as far as china and the extra trips that are made from home to work, increases more injury and deaths in accidents caused by more Trucks and cars in the roads. (The accidents are good for business too! More medical, medicine, car and equipment and materials are sold. More things smash and crash, more conflicts and wars, more violence and crimes are good for business too!).

FOOD POISONING

They have sacrificed the quality of production over the quantity to benefit from producing and selling more of the cheap and unhealthy food.

Just like the policy of the shipment of the productions thousands miles away and back to cheaply produce products, that causes more death in traffic accidents, the policy of the cheap production of food has also caused thousands deaths and sufferings.

They have increased the amount of none healthy food such as none organic, hormonized, engineered foods, corn syrup, fat, sugar, caffeine, nicotine, alcohol, tobacco, drugs and even crack heroin! They have expanded franchised food suppliers and food producer's companies (That they have shares in and profit from) to produce cheap junk food and feeding the public cheaply by unhealthy food that are high in sugar, caffeine, fat and chemicals that sickens people, which increases the sales of medicine, medical and gym equipment, and insurance. Thousands of people get sick and depressed or die for consuming unhealthy junk food sold by the groups with more assets who control franchised junk food and meat suppliers.

AUCTIONING OUT DEMOCRACY TO PRIVATE ENTITIES

The majority of the population has to work for private companies whose authorities are not elected in office democratically. Leaders in command of private companies, who are not elected in office, dictate rules and adjust the public salaries without people having any voice in the making of rules or electing any of them in office. No employee has a say in the decision making of the company's board. The board members and the chief executives are not elected by public vote.

Auctioning out the Banking and production and services to privates and allow them to control all aspects of the public life (Work, housing, investment, loaning, production and services) by the savings of the private entities which are not elected democratically has turned the democratic establishment into an authoritarian state.

A few none-elected individuals with wealth and savings are given authority in the Government and they are given authority by private companies to make rules for the public. (Private Bankers of the Federal Bank and Executives of companies).

HARMING THE ENVIRONMENT, ANIMAL AND PLANTS

The officials, who have committed Conspiracies that have defrauded the United States' laws of the Constitution and have caused the tortures and deaths of thousands of the citizens of the United States and the people of other 194 nations, have also committed crimes against animals, plants and the environment of the United States as well as the World!

The corrupted policies of the corrupted officials, who are corrupted in mind by their corrupted ideological belief, have tortured and harmed animals, plants and the environment of the United States by the unnecessary shipments of production thousands of miles away that have caused more pollution by the increase in the length of transporting products and resources thousands miles back and forth. Ships and Trucks use tons of Oil and emit heat and toxic gases that warms the climate causing species to go extinct, severing earthquakes, tsunamis, hurricanes, and fire storms and killing more of plants, trees, birds and animals to build roads, ships, equipment and cars to transport the products and resources thousands of miles back and forth. This is the Major Fraud not only against the United States, but a Major Fraud against Life!

Not only more U.S. citizens suffer and die, but also animals, plants and the Planet itself suffer and die as the result of policies set to benefit less than % 0.001th of the world population. (Not considering the Wales, Dolphins, Dogs, Corals, parrots, and horses of course).

Officials' taking Oath to the Bible is not a joke. They do believe in the Bible and its Armageddon! They don't mind if the U.S. Citizens, its animals and Plants and the Planet Earth itself is destroyed because the destructions would simply fulfill their Bible's prophecies that they think will not be avoidable!

Their Bible says that the destruction of the world is going to happen by those who have their hands on the Bible and if the destruction of the world happens to happen by such hands, it is because of what their God wants! (They don't mind setting policies that destroys life because it matches their ideology that says the life is to be destroyed! Wars would have to start from a small nation to destroy everyone and everything to fulfill the ideology!)

The life is to be destroyed and they don't mind at all because it just confirms their belief in such destruction of such prophecy!

Their policy of stealing from others has turned many nations into enemy of each other destroying and polluting tons of the Earth resources into weapons used in wars or building thousands of nuclear bombs that could destroy life many times over! The U.S. alone made over 7,000 nuclear bombs that is a threat to the Earth! It could destroy the Earth many times over! The Conspiracy of the officials in the office, that is based on securing their own assets, interests and profits, and is based on securing their belief of destroying life (Either destroying the life of a person as a slave beating him in the back, slaughtering Bison for their skins, or cutting trees and build concrete roads and building and polluting) have created hostile polices toward many other nations causing many nations to waste much of their G.D.P on weaponry and nuclear bombs that slowly destroys animals, plants and the environment and it could destroy life and Earth if a nuclear war is triggered!

DEFRAUDING THE EDUCATION

Another Major Fraud against the people of the United States is defrauding people's education!

They train people to commit fraud and perjury in order to become a politician in public schools and they confuse people's mind from youth by teaching them contradictions, hatred, and racism. They corrupt the young mind by teaching them how to lie to public. Not only they corrupt youth by religious ideology to be selfish and hate many other groups of people, but also they corrupt them from youth by teaching them to commit fraud and perjury at public schools! They literally teach students to lie to public about facts!

The Plaintiff K, this writer, was taught by Jacksonville Community College to lie to public in order to become a politician! He was directed by the college's text book of Macroeconomics/Microeconomics, to lie to the Citizens of the United States saying that the economy was doing very well if the economy was really doing bad! He was required

TO LIE to people and tell them that the economy was doing well if it really was doing bad reasoning that if people knew the truth that the economy was doing bad, people would not spend their money on products and as the result the economy would get worse. Authorities thinking of themselves as superior to others and they are allowed to keep secret from the public because they are raised to believe that they are established authority by the power of God and that they are the shepherd who lead the rest of the people whom they think of as their sheep!

Just like the stories in their Bible that is not based on facts, they create commands of their own and value their commands as fact!

They are raised from young age to praise their own ideology, which praises them above others and tells them to treat others as low people or subjects! Their minds are corrupted from young age at religious or public schools to accept lie and contradictions as true and fact and they are taught to lie instead of telling the true! (The lie and contradictions of: "showing the other cheek if stricken and love your enemy which contradicts with other religious and Governmental teaching of fighting the enemy by killing their men and taking their women and children!).

The minds are confused with lies and contradictions so they are easily controlled and directed by religious leaders who have infiltrated in the Government to use and promote the religious ideology to have access to authority to gain people's wealth and savings!

Their incorrect economic policies of shipping works overseas, print money out of paper and out of NOTHING, increasing the cost of housings, stealing the intellectuals and resources of other countries creating poverty, violence, and crimes, wars and terrorism, which have caused the bad economy and has harmed people, are to be corrected by the INCORRECT information given to people!

They correct their own incorrect and corrupt criminal actions with further incorrect, corrupt, and criminal actions!

Exactly following their Bible dual teaching that says it is OK to Kidnap others and keep as slaves but it is a sin if you do it to your own tribes! The double standard of humanity sickens the mind from childhood when children are told that they are chosen by God on Earth and others are to be their slaves!

The Conspiracy to defraud the United States economically, politically, socially and culturally, has been intentional because it has been ideological! In order to steal from millions of people, they intentionally and systematically designed policies that harmed millions of people internally and internationally. The corrupt policies of the corrupt politicians are drawn from their corrupt religious ideology that has been corrupting the human mind for more than 3,500 years and caused the thousands years of human sufferings in their religious ideological wars.

Such crimes would have not had happened if officials had not made any commitments to commit such crimes by taking Oaths to their biblical belief, which threatens to harm many citizens of the United States. And such crimes would not have happened if officials had not praised the criminals, George Washington, who committed the very same crime that was required from them to commit!

In the ideological book of Bible, judges, Senators and Presidents, have been swearing their loyalty to follow the gross commands of such ideology for the past 244 years!

They have committed themselves to the threats to commit the crimes that they were required to commit in their Bible by taking loyalty Oath to the threats.

And they have committed themselves to commit the crimes that they are required to commit in the Bible by praising heroes like George Washington or General Lee, who have committed the crimes that were required from them to commit by their Bible.

That is why they intentionally caused hardship on the people of the United States and they knowingly have caused thousands to be killed or to die as the results of their selfish policies that primarily benefited themselves and their groups of friends!

They require from children to be nationalistic, patriotic, and believe in one faith and country only and they are taught that others, like Muslims, are to be harmed!

They are teaching them to lie and asking them to be patriotic to the lies and harm others who think differently or appear differently from them. They corrupt people from youth at schools teaching those lies, hatred and racism.

CHILD ABUSE AND KIDNAPPING

The officials have committed child abuse and Kidnapping because they had their hands on the child abuse and Kidnapping threats that are made in the Bible in a public office, and because they praised or worked under the flag of George Washington who committed child abuse and Kidnapping, thus they are a complicit in all of the Kidnappings and the child abuses committed by State officials, Priest or individuals because such crimes would not had happened if:

1. The high rank officials had not promoted the religion that promotes child abuse and the kidnapping and if:
2. The high rank officials had not promoted the figures who had committed child abuse and the Kidnapping.

Thousands of children were separated from their families or sexually, physically, or emotionally being abused directly by the hands of judges, priests, presidents, senators and other officials who have their hands on the threats made in the Bible or under the flag of Washington. They have set malicious rules and policies to fulfill their Oath that is made into malicious rules and commands, and they have obstructed justice by dismissing this case to literally obstruct the justice and obscure their Conspiracy and therefore they are responsible for the Tort they caused on millions of people including Mr. K, this writer. (And Native Americans, African Americans, and other families including immigrants who are separated from their children).

Mr. K. was forced to quit collage. He couldn't have accepted to commit Perjury in order to be educated and being hired in office. He lost the opportunity of receiving a degree that could have enabled him to be hired earning more income. He was also beaten and jailed many times unreasonably and one time detained in mental hospital without having access to due process of law for a month just because of what he wrote! The court forced him into living in the street, he was expelled from Universities, colleges, grocery stores, public libraries and many other private and public buildings for him looking "homeless" or for him expressing his grievances against the Government. He was also denied employments on the bases of him being issued a warrant (Wrongfully), and for him being defamed wrongfully for abusing his child and for him being restrained to visit his child or for being thought of as a "pagan" national and a "none-believer". Mr. K. had home and own business yet pushed into homeless because he was treated by the racist religious based rule derived from Bible which states that two witness testimony are valued as truth under oath and is enough to satisfy the claim and thus enough to execute a sentence against the accused! (Thousands are wrongfully imprisoned or punished only on bases of the rule of two witness testimony that is derived from Bible).

The officials also harmed the plaintiff, his child; TK and the mother of his child by restraining him from even visiting them!

The officials, (With corporation with Corporations and Churches) have:

1. Destabilized the country Mr. K. was raised in and:

2. They help bombing, burning, and destroying his family business at least 3 times and:

3. They stole the wealth, the resources, the intellectuals and the wealthy people of the country Mr. K. lived in making him poor forcing him into migration to suffer and:

4. They poisoned the democratic elected leader of his born country and created a coup de ta by bribing mobs in the country Mr. K. lived, and they appointed a dictator and directed him to burn down Mr. K's family business, and they collaborated with another country dictator

(Saddam Hossain), to attack the county Mr. K. lived in and they destroyed his family business once again and:

5. They have backed the islamists and directed them to eliminate none-believers by murdering Mr. K. friends and relatives, and:

6. They have backed islamists to torture and imprison Mr. K. overseas, and:

7. They have tortured Mr. K. by Kidnaping his child inside the U.S. (Taking revenge against him for writing against authorities wrongfully accusing him of abandoning his child) and:

8. They have detained him unjustly and:

9. They expel Mr. K. from public places and:

10. They caused other private and public entities to expel him from places or from hiring him or causing him to be fired for him being considered none believer, being from a "pagan" nation who spoke the truth and did not follow the corrupt rules of the public and private entities. (For example he was expelled from courts for talking against the court and he was expelled from public university for talking against the Bible). Also:

11. The police and marshal provided protection for rich by protecting their property and they ignored the safety of k's life and the protection of his child and family.

12. They sent him away issuing a trespassing for him while allowed the child to remain with kidnappers in their house even when he had the custody.

13. The police and marshal did not provide safety for him while they do for those who pay. (He had asked police and marshals for protection but because he didn't have money to pay for protection he was sent away).

14. There was no room in Shelter and he was sent away from there also. He wasn't allowed to enter many public and private building including Federal court building!

15. He is banned to visit his offspring.

16. He is banned to visit his partner and the mother of his child for live and therefore:

17. He was not allowed to reproduce offspring by public and private. (He was restrained to meet the mother of his child without her having any objection. And he was banned from dating or

talking other females at private and public entities).

All above is an example of the Governments' commitment committing Genocide by the book.

Made in the USA
Monee, IL
07 August 2020